Only in California

Recipes that capture the spirit and lifestyle which make California so unique

Children's Home Society of California

Edited by:
Joyce Hyde and Sue Bubnack

Children's Home Society of California (CHS) is a private, nonprofit, multi-service agency offering services based upon a historical mission to protect the well-being of children. The purpose of CHS is to respond to community needs by developing and providing high quality child welfare services.

CHS is one of the most diversified child welfare agencies in the United States, and this diversity allows us to assist children at many different levels of need. Over ten thousand children benefit directly each year through CHS programs. These programs include: adoption, child care, foster care and group home care, family support and shelter care services.

Profits received through the sale of this book will directly benefit the children and families in these programs.

First Edition   10,000 copies   September, 1989
Second Edition   10,000 copies   October, 1989

ISBN: 0-9622898-0-9
Library of Congress Card Catalog: 89-061386

Printed by
WIMMER BROTHERS
Memphis   Dallas

INTRODUCTION

Throughout the history of our country, the mystique and promise of California has beckoned adventurous pioneers and visitors to its borders.

The cornucopia of scenery in California can stimulate the senses and peak the emotions of all who care to observe. Only in California can one witness the daring, excitement and passion of sizzling southern beaches and hot, colorful deserts; travel a few miles and savor the charm, serenity and elegance of quiet, verdant farmland or restored missions; and within a short distance experience the majesty of the Redwood Forest, snowswept mountains and the Golden Gate Bridge or just enjoy the splendor of Hollywood or a trip to the San Diego Zoo.

The diversity of backgrounds of the citizens of California makes it an All-American state. The rich cultural heritage, myriad lifestyles, cutting-edge attitudes and traditional values of the population make California the true melting pot of the West.

The best of America is here . . . . . . in California!

ONLY IN CALIFORNIA, a new cookbook compiled and published to raise funds to benefit Children's Home Society of California (CHS), captures the spirit and lifestyle which makes California so unique.

Children's Home Society of California offers vulnerable families and children in California a multi-service program responsive to the needs of local communities and tailored to local resources.

ACKNOWLEDGEMENTS

NORDSTROM, INC.

ESHA RESEARCH
The Food Processor II
Nutrition and Diet Analysis System

CALIFORNIA TOURISM CORPORATION

DEDICATION

This book is dedicated to our friend,
Ruth Kulis,
with love.

*Her good humor, leadership and
support served as our inspiration.*

COMMITTEE CO-CHAIRMEN

Sue Bubnack
Joyce Hyde

STEERING COMMITTEE

Benella Bouldin
Marilyn Desmond
Nancy McDougal
Pat Prickett
Diane Rogers
Ann Scanlin
Joan Thorne
Carmi Vescelus
Dorothy Fitzgerald
Ruth Kulis
Gloria Slata
Lori Schneider
Diane Easton

ARTISTIC COORDINATOR

Gayle Brownstein

SELECTION COMMITTEE

Sharon Cutri
Brooke Peterson
Diane Murdoch

TYPING AND EDITING

Sharon Cutri

COMPUTER TYPING AND EDITING

Nancy McDougal

*For freely giving of their time and expertise,
we also wish to thank:*

Ethel Lichtman
Charles Hyde
Bruce McDougal

Table of Contents

◊ *Symbol denotes recipes with nutritional information. The nutritional values are figured on the largest number of servings indicated in the yields.*

Appetizers

APPETIZERS

Wines matched with appetizers are usually lighter and younger than those used to complement a main dish. Choose from the "light to mid-range" categories. Of course, Sparkling Wine goes with almost anything. A few examples:

Chinese — Gewurztraminer, with egg rolls, won tons and most things; Johannisberg Riesling also works.

Italian — Zinfandel, Barbera and Sauvignon (or Fume) Blanc for the light to mid-range foods in spiciness; Zinfandel and Petite Sirah for the richest red sauces, sausages. The same works for American barbecue.

All-American — Sauvignon Blanc for the lighter dishes and meats; inexpensive varietals (Emerald and Grey Riesling, Sylvaner, Green Hungarian, French Colombard and White Zinfandel) for chips and dip and junk food; Gamay, Barbera and Zinfandel for meats; White Zinfandel or rose for ham.

French — Sauvignon Blanc and Zinfandel with the pate; Gamay Beaujolais, Barbera and Zinfandel with breads and cheeses; Johannisberg Riesling with fruit; Chardonnay with crab legs, fresh shrimp or other seafood.

Pickled Shrimp

1. Place frozen shrimp in boiling water. Bring back to boil. Boil only one minute.

2. Rinse, drain and chill.

3. Alternate layers of shrimp and onion rings in a bowl. Mix remaining ingredients together and pour over the shrimp.

4. Refrigerate 6 hours or more. Pickled shrimp will keep several days in the refrigerator, covered tightly. Yield: 6 to 8 servings.

2 **pounds medium to large frozen shrimp (peeled and deveined)**
2 **medium onions, sliced in rings**
¾ **cup vegetable oil**
¾ **cup white vinegar**
1 **tablespoon honey**
¾ **teaspoon salt**
¾ **teaspoon celery seed**
4 **tablespoons capers with juice**

Marinated Spiced Shrimp and Mushrooms

1. Combine all ingredients and marinate, covered, in refrigerator. It is best if prepared a day or two ahead of time.

2. Serve with cocktail picks as hors d'oeuvres, or as first course, served on a bed of lettuce or in scallop shells. Yield: 20 to 25 servings.

3 **pounds shrimp, cooked, peeled, and deveined**
2 **pounds mushrooms**
1 **cup vegetable oil**
1 **cup vinegar**
4 **onions, sliced**
10 **bay leaves, whole**
2 **tablespoons sugar**
4 **tablespoons whole allspice**
2 **cloves garlic, crushed**
¼ **tablespoon each of savory, basil, thyme, tarragon**
salt and pepper to taste

Shrimp and Olive Appetizer

36 large shrimp, cooked,
cooled, peeled, and
deveined
1 (16 ounce) can large
pitted olives
36 toothpicks
½ cup mayonnaise
⅛ teaspoon dry mustard
3 tablespoons catsup
½ medium dill pickle,
chopped
2 teaspoons parsley,
chopped
1 hard-boiled egg,
chopped
salt and pepper to taste

1. Drain olives. Put shrimp around each olive and fasten with toothpick. Arrange on dish.

2. Mix the remaining ingredients together. Use as a dip for the shrimp.

3. Can be made early in the day; cover shrimp and olives tightly in the refrigerator. Yield: 36 appetizers.

Shrimp Boats

1 pound shrimp meat,
cooked and chopped
(can substitute fresh
crab)
3 tablespoons lemon juice
½ cup imitation mayon-
naise
2 tablespoons parsley,
finely chopped
2 tablespoons chives or
scallions, finely chopped
1 tablespoon fresh basil,
finely chopped
salt and pepper to taste
3-4 heads Belgian endive,
washed and patted dry

1. Mix shrimp meat, lemon juice, mayonnaise, parsley, chives and basil together. Season with salt and pepper to taste. (Can be made ahead and kept in an air-tight container for one day.)

2. Separate endive leaves carefully. Arrange on serving platter in circular pattern and fill each leaf with a spoonful of the shrimp mixture. Garnish center of platter with tomato roses or fresh flowers. Yield: 15 to 20 servings.

◊ Nutritional information per serving:

Calories 46	Fat ....2 g	Iron ....0.9 mg
Protein ....6 g	Cholesterol ....41 mg	Potassium ....133 mg
Carbohydrates ....2 g	Calcium ....31 mg	Sodium ....74 mg

Mexican Shrimp Cocktail

1. Mix all ingredients in a glass bowl with a wooden spoon.

2. Refrigerate for several hours.

3. Serve on a bed of lettuce or as an appetizer served with crackers. Yield: 6 servings.

¾ cup cooked small shrimp

2 medium lemons, juice only

2 medium limes, juice only

1 cup tomatoes, peeled and diced

1-2 fresh small hot green chiles, seeded and diced

1 medium onion, finely chopped

¼ cup vegetable oil

1 teaspoon oregano

1 teaspoon minced fresh cilantro (or more to taste)

¼ teaspoon garlic salt

◊ Nutritional information per serving:

Calories 119	Fat .... 10 g	Iron .... 0.77 mg
Protein .... 4 g	Cholesterol .... 28 mg	Potassium .... 161 mg
Carbohydrates .... 5 g	Calcium .... 22 mg	Sodium .... 30 mg

Onion Mushroom Spread

1. Saute onions, mushrooms and garlic in hot oil in large skillet over medium heat for 2 minutes. Remove from heat and stir in cream cheese.

2. Pour into food processor and blend until smooth. Add Parmesan cheese, parsley and soy sauce and blend. Pour into serving dish; cover and refrigerate three hours or overnight.

3. Spread on French bread slices and garnish with black olives. Yield: 6 to 10 servings.

½ cup chopped onion

½ pound fresh mushrooms, chopped

1 clove garlic, minced

1 tablespoon olive oil

1 (8 ounce) package cream cheese, softened and quartered

¼ cup Parmesan cheese, grated

¼ cup minced fresh parsley

2 tablespoons soy sauce

1 loaf French bread baguette, sliced thinly black olive slices

Curry Cheese Spread

2 (8 ounce) packages
cream cheese
2 cups shredded sharp
Cheddar cheese
½ cup chopped chutney
2 tablespoons mayon-
naise
⅓ cup chopped green
onions
2 cloves garlic, crushed
2 teaspoons curry pow-
der, or to taste
1 teaspoon dry mustard

Optional Garnishes:
⅓ cup additional chutney
coconut, flaked
peanuts, chopped
raisins
¼ cup sliced almonds

1. Blend the cream cheese (a little bit at a time) and Cheddar in food processor with blade until blended smooth and with uniform color. Add chutney, mayonnaise, green onions, garlic, curry, dry mustard. Blend well.

2. Pour mixture in a mold, lined with plastic wrap. Refrigerate for at least 3 hours.

3. Before serving, unmold. Garnish with optional toppings for color. Serve with crackers. Yield: 15 to 20 servings.

Shrimp Dip or Spread

2 (8 ounce) packages
cream cheese
½ cup chopped celery
½ cup chopped green
onions
½ cup mayonnaise
3 cans medium shrimp (4
cans if small shrimp),
frozen or fresh shrimp
may be used, chopped
1 package unflavored
gelatin
1 (10½ ounce) can tomato
soup

1. Blend together cream cheese, celery, onion and mayonnaise. Add shrimp, set aside.

2. Dissolve gelatin in soup in small saucepan; heat until bubbly. Pour warm soup into creamed cheese-shrimp mixture; fold gently. Pour into a mold if desired, or use as a spread. Chill for at least 6 hours.

3. Serve with crackers.

Note: Crab may be substituted. Serve on a bed of lettuce as a salad, or as a mold or spread.

Salmon Party Log

1. Mix all ingredients, except walnuts and parsley, and chill.

2. Form mixture into a 2 inch diameter log.

3. Mix nuts and parsley together and roll log in mixture.

4. Serve with crackers.

1 (16 ounce) can salmon, well-drained, bones and skin removed, flaked
1 (8 ounce) package cream cheese, softened
1 tablespoon lemon juice
2 teaspoons grated onion
1 teaspoon horseradish
1 teaspoon liquid smoke
¼ teaspoon salt (if desired)
½ cup chopped walnuts
2 tablespoons chopped parsley

Pecan-Coated Cheese Ball

1. Let cheeses warm to room temperature, then beat together until light and fluffy and well blended. Add onion and garlic.

2. Shape and roll into a ball, using plastic spatula. Wrap in waxed paper and chill for several hours.

3. Roll in chopped nuts until well-coated. Keep in refrigerator until needed.

4. Low-fat cream cheese may be substituted.

5. Serve with crackers, or with cocktail-size rye or sourdough bread.

1 (8 ounce) package cream cheese
1 (5 ounce) jar processed sharp Cheddar cheese spread
4 ounces aged bleu cheese, crumbled
1 small onion, finely minced
1 clove garlic, minced
½ cup chopped pecans or walnuts

Hot Mushroom Turnovers

1 (8 ounce) package
  cream cheese, softened
1½ cups flour
 ½ cup butter, softened
 3 tablespoons butter
 ½ pound mushrooms,
  minced
 1 large onion, minced
 ¼ cup sour cream
 1 teaspoon salt
 ¼ teaspoon thyme
 2 tablespoons flour
 1 egg, beaten

1. In a large bowl with mixer at medium speed, beat cream cheese, flour and ½ cup butter until smooth. Shape into ball and wrap with cloth. Refrigerate for 1 hour.

2. In a skillet over medium heat, melt 3 tablespoons butter and cook mushrooms and onions until tender, stirring occasionally. Stir in sour cream, salt, thyme, and 2 tablespoons flour. Set aside.

3. On floured surface with floured rolling pin, roll half of dough ⅛ inch thick. With a floured 2¾ inch round cookie cutter, cut as many circles as possible. Re-roll and repeat until all the dough has been used.

4. Preheat oven to 450°. On half of each dough circle, place a teaspoon of mushroom mixture. Brush edges of circle with some egg, fold over. Press edges firmly with a fork to seal. Prick tops. Place turnovers on greased cookie sheet, brush with remaining egg.

5. Bake at 450° for 12 to 14 minutes until golden brown. Yield: 42 turnovers.

Little Cream Puffs with Chicken-Nut Salad Filling

1. Heat oven to 450°. Lightly grease a baking sheet.

2. Heat water to boiling in a saucepan. Add butter or margarine and stir until melted. Add flour all at once and stir constantly and vigorously until mixture leaves the sides of the pan and forms a ball. This should take about 1 minute. Remove from heat and allow to cool slightly.

3. Add eggs, one at a time, beating until mixture is smooth and velvety.

4. Drop from the tip of a teaspoon onto the baking sheet, keeping the balls 2 inches apart. They should be the size of walnuts.

5. Bake 10 minutes at 450°. Reduce heat to 350° and bake for 10 to 15 minutes longer. Remove from oven and allow to cool slowly away from drafts. When cool, cut off the tops with a sharp knife and scoop out any pieces of soft dough. Fill the puffs with the chicken-nut mixture. Yield: 18 puffs.

½ cup water
¼ cup butter or margarine
½ cup flour
 2 eggs

Chicken-Nut Filling:
1. Combine chicken with almonds, mayonnaise, sour cream, lemon juice, and salt and pepper to taste.

2. Optional: Garnish with chopped parsley or basil, green or red grapes. For a different flavor, add basil to the mayonnaise and substitute lime juice for lemon juice.

Chicken-Nut Filling:
2½ **cups finely minced cooked chicken**
⅔ **cup almonds, chopped**
½ **cup mayonnaise**
⅓ **cup sour cream**
 2 **tablespoons lemon juice salt and pepper to taste**

Chicken Wings Mandarin

15-20   chicken wings
 1 cup cornstarch
 2 eggs, well beaten
 ¼ teaspoon seasoned salt
    dash garlic powder
    milk, as needed
 ¾ cup sugar
 ¼ cup water
 ½ cup Japanese vinegar
    (can substitute white
    vinegar)
    soy sauce, few drops
    catsup, few drops to
    give sauce orange color

1. Cut wings into 3 sections at the joints. Discard the tips (or use for making soup). Take one of the bones out of the middle section of the wing and scrape and push the meat to one end of the bone. Push and scrape the meat to one end of the bone on the remaining section of the wing. They should resemble a small drumstick. (Note: If you don't want to take time to scrape the wings, you can buy the upper part of the wing in packages, called "drummettes".)

2. Mix cornstarch, seasoned salt, eggs, and garlic powder. Add enough milk to make a batter of medium consistency. Stir lightly. Coat wings with batter and deep fry in hot oil until slightly browned. Drain.

3. Combine sugar, water, vinegar, soy sauce and catsup. Dip wings in sauce and place in a flat pan. Pour remainder of the sauce over wings.

4. Bake at 350° about 30 minutes or until sauce is absorbed. Baste and turn wings frequently. Yield: 8-10 servings.

Note: For easier clean-up, line pan with foil before placing wings in it. Remove the wings while hot to serving platter. If left in the baking pan until cooled, it will stick to the foil.

Parmesan Chicken Wings

1. Cut tips of wings and save for soup. Melt butter in a large foil-lined baking pan in 425° oven.

2. Mix flour, salt, cheese, paprika, and oregano in medium-sized bowl. Dip wings in buttermilk; roll in flour mixture, then gently roll in melted butter and arrange in pan.

3. Bake for 45 to 60 minutes at 425°, or until very brown and crispy. Yield: 6 to 8 servings.

4 **pounds chicken wings (about 32)**
½ **cup butter**
1 **cup flour**
2½ **teaspoons salt**
½ **cup grated Parmesan cheese**
½ **teaspoon paprika**
½ **teaspoon oregano**
⅔ **cup buttermilk**

Crab Bread

1. Slice off the top of the bread round and hollow out the inside, saving the bread and the top.

2. Mix together all remaining ingredients and place mixture in the hollowed out bread bowl. Cover with reserved top. Wrap in heavy foil and place on a baking sheet. Bake at 250° for 3 hours.

3. Before serving, cut up the reserved bread into cubes. Place bread bowl on a serving plate and surround with bread cubes. Yield: 12 to 15 servings.

1 **round unsliced loaf of sourdough bread**
3 **(8 ounce) packages cream cheese**
2 **(6½ ounce) cans crab, drained**
1 **(4 ounce) can green chiles, chopped**
4 **green onions, chopped**
4 **tablespoons parsley, chopped**
Worcestershire sauce to taste
hot pepper sauce to taste

Variation: Substitute 2 cans chopped clams, drained, in place of the crab. Add 1 small can chopped black olives.

Crab Wontons

36 small wonton skin
squares
1 (6½ ounce) can
crabmeat, drained
2 tablespoons green
onions, minced
2 tablespoons Parmesan
cheese
2 tablespoons bread
crumbs
1 (8 ounce) package
cream cheese
vegetable oil

Variation on Filling:
8 ounces cream cheese
16 water chestnuts,
chopped
½ teaspoon salt
½ teaspoon Worcester-
shire sauce
2 tablespoons sesame
seeds
6½ ounces crab
6 teaspoons cilantro,
chopped
½ teaspoon ginger,
pressed through garlic
press

1. Blend crabmeat, cream cheese, Parmesan cheese, onions and bread crumbs until smooth (do not use blender or food processor).

2. Put a heaping teaspoonful in center of wonton skin, fold corners to overlap. Seal edges with water.

3. Deep fry at 375° in one inch of vegetable oil until golden. Yield: 36 appetizers.

Stuffed Mushrooms

1. Fry bacon and remove from pan. Drain bacon grease from pan.

2. Remove mushroom stems and chop. In same skillet, melt butter. Add bacon, green pepper, onion, garlic and mushroom stems. Saute 2 to 3 minutes. Remove from heat.

3. Add cream cheese and mayonnaise. Stir over low heat until cheese is melted. Add salt, pepper and hot pepper sauce.

4. Stuff mushrooms with cheese mixture. Top each with a sprinkle of Parmesan cheese and bread crumbs.

5. Bake at 350° for 10 to 12 minutes. Yield: 30 appetizers.

½ pound bacon, diced
30 large mushrooms
1 green bell pepper, chopped
1 onion, chopped
2 garlic cloves, minced
salt, pepper and hot pepper sauce to taste
2 tablespoons butter
1 (8 ounce) package cream cheese
2 tablespoons mayonnaise
seasoned bread crumbs
Parmesan cheese

Fried Cauliflower Appetizer

1. Break cauliflower into flowerets and parboil for 5 minutes until crunchy-tender. Dip in cold water to refresh, drain well.

2. Prepare batter by mixing eggs, flour, salt, pepper, vinegar, oil and parsley.

3. Heat vegetable oil in frying pan to depth of 2 inches. Dip cauliflower into batter and fry until golden brown. Drain on paper towels. Transfer to serving platter. Yield: 8 to 12 servings.

4 small heads cauliflower
4 eggs, lightly beaten
2 cups flour
salt and fresh ground pepper to taste
2 tablespoons vinegar
1 tablespoon vegetable oil
chopped parsley
vegetable oil for frying

Optional: Serve a horseradish sauce or a ranch style dressing for dipping.

Tiropetes (Filo Dough with Cream Cheese Filling)

1 (8 ounce) package
   cream cheese
3 ounces Swiss cheese,
   grated
1 egg
1 tablespoon finely
   minced parsley
7 sheets filo dough (keep
   covered with damp tea
   towel while working, to
   avoid drying out)
½ cup butter, melted in 9
   inch pie pan

1. In a food processor or mixer combine the two cheeses. Add egg and mix until well blended. Add parsley.

2. Lay out one sheet of filo dough and, using your hand, lightly cover with melted butter. Cut into 3 inch wide strips, about 14 inches long.

3. Place one teaspoon cheese filling in one corner of the strip and fold over itself to make a triangle. Continue folding over and over until you reach the end of the strip of dough. Place on ungreased cookie sheet and brush tops with a little butter.

4. Bake at 375° for 10 minutes or until triangles are golden brown, both bottom and top. Remove to serving plate. Yield: 36 appetizers.

Shrimp Puffs

1 package butter flaked
   rolls (in a tube)
½ cup light cream (half
   and half)
1 egg
½ teaspoon salt
¼ teaspoon dill
4 dashes hot sauce
2 green onions, minced
6 ounces frozen tiny
   shrimp
½ cup finely shredded
   Swiss cheese
   paprika
   small muffin tins

1. Spray muffin cups with non-stick cooking spray for easy clean-up. Separate rolls, then separate each roll into 3 or 4 rounds. Place one round into each muffin cup.

2. Beat cream, egg, salt, dill, and hot sauce until well mixed. Add onions, shrimp and cheese to beaten mixture and blend well.

3. Spoon mixture into muffin cups, dust with paprika and bake at 375° for 20 minutes. Yield: 24 servings.

Note: This recipe can be made ahead and frozen. If frozen, place in oven at 350° and reheat for 15 minutes or until hot.

Party Pizza Rounds

1. Remove casings from sausage and cook beef and sausage until well cooked. Drain well. Add spices and mix well. Cut cheese into small chunks; add to meat mixture and heat until melted.

2. Spread mixture on party rounds Place on a cookie sheet; broil until brown and hot all the way through or heat at 350° for about 10 minutes until browned. Yield: 4 to 6 dozen.

1 **pound ground beef**
1 **pound hot pork sausage or Italian sausage**
½ **teaspoon oregano**
½ **teaspoon onion or garlic powder**
1 **pound pasteurized processed cheese spread**
2 **packages of party round bread, rye, onion or your favorite**

Optional: For a light meal, spread mixture on English muffins and bake.

Note: May be frozen on a cookie sheet, then transferred to a plastic bag or covered container. Thaw slightly before cooking or re-heating.

Cheese Capers

1. Mix all ingredients together in a large bowl. Spread on open face English muffins and place on a cookie sheet. Sprinkle with Parmesan cheese. Cut into quarters.

2. Bake at 350° for 15 minutes, or place under broiler until cheese melts and is bubbly. Yield: 32 pieces.

2 **cups grated Cheddar cheese (or 1 cup Cheddar, 1 cup mozzarella)**
½ **cup mayonnaise**
¼ **cup finely sliced green onions**
8-10 **green olives, finely chopped**
1 **tablespoon finely chopped pimentos**
1 **tablespoon chopped capers**
Parmesan cheese
8 **English muffin halves**

Note: Cheese Capers may be frozen before sprinkling with Parmesan cheese.

Spinach Puffs

2 (10 ounce) packages
frozen chopped spinach
2 cups crushed herb
seasoned stuffing mix
1 cup grated Parmesan
cheese
dash of nutmeg
6 eggs, beaten
¾ cup butter, softened

1. Thaw spinach, drain and squeeze. Mix spinach with remaining ingredients.

2. Shape mixture into 65 balls. Refrigerate for one hour or more.

3. Bake 10 to 15 minutes at 350°. Remove from oven and drain on paper towels.

4. Serve on a plate with toothpicks and Mustard Sauce. Yield: 65 puffs.

Note: Best if made the night before. Can be made ahead and frozen; thaw in refrigerator before baking.

Mustard Sauce:

½ cup dry mustard (use ⅓
cup if you prefer less
mustard)
½ cup white vinegar
½ cup honey
2 egg yolks

1. Combine mustard and vinegar in bowl. Cover and let stand overnight at room temperature.

2. Next day: Combine mustard with honey and stirred egg yolks in a small saucepan. Simmer, stirring occasionally until thickened.

3. Allow to cool to room temperature; serve. Yield: About 1½ cups.

Note: Mustard Sauce is very good served with ham.

Hot Artichoke-Cheese Dip

1. Grease a 7½x11½ inch baking dish. Preheat oven to 350°.

2. Chop artichokes coarsely and spread evenly into dish. Layer chiles over top of artichokes. Carefully spread mayonnaise over chiles. Sprinkle Cheddar cheese over all.

3. Bake 15 minutes at 350°.

4. Serve with tortilla chips. May be served either hot or cold, but best hot. Yield: 6 to 8 servings.

1 **(8½ ounce) can artichoke hearts, drained**
1 **(6 ounce) jar marinated artichokes, drained**
1 **(4 ounce) can diced green chiles**
6 **tablespoons mayonnaise**
2 **cups Cheddar cheese, shredded**
tortilla chips

Mushroom Dill Dip

1. Mix together and refrigerate at least 4 hours.

2. Serve with fresh vegetables for dipping. Can be made a day ahead. Yield: 4 to 6 servings.

½ **cup imitation mayonnaise**
½ **cup lowfat yogurt**
½ **teaspoon fresh or dried dill**
1 **cup raw mushrooms, finely chopped**
1 **large clove garlic, minced**
1 **teaspoon fresh lemon juice**

◊ Nutritional information per serving:

Calories 60	Fat .... 4 g	Iron .... 0.07 mg
Protein .... 1 g	Cholesterol .... 7 mg	Potassium .... 53 mg
Carbohydrates .... 4 g	Calcium .... 37 mg	Sodium .... 114 mg

Bagna Cauda (Hot Italian Dip)

3 (2 ounce) cans ancho-
   vies, chopped
1 head of garlic (2
   ounces), finely chopped
1 cup olive oil
1 cup butter
2 loaves French bread,
   sliced

Vegetables for Dipping:
   (cut into bite-size
   pieces) zucchini sticks,
   carrot sticks, red peppers, mushrooms,
   finocchio (fennel),
   cauliflower, cabbage
   chunks

1. Combine all ingredients except the bread and vegetables and simmer for 5 to 10 minutes or until anchovies dissolve into a paste. Serve in chafing dish to keep warm.

2. Stir occasionally to keep the anchovies mixed, as they tend to sink to the bottom of the dish.

3. Spread on French bread or use as a dip for vegetables. Yield: 15 to 20 servings.

Note: Also may be used as a sauce over pasta.

Baked Crab Dip

1 (8 ounce) package
   cream cheese
1 (6½ ounce) can
   crabmeat or imitation
   crab (fresh, frozen, or
   canned)
2 tablespoons finely
   grated onion
½ teaspoon prepared
   horseradish
3 tablespoons mayon-
   naise
   salt and white pepper to
   taste
   dash Worcestershire
   sauce
   white wine
⅓ cup toasted almonds,
   thinly sliced

1. Combine all ingredients except the almonds. Place in an oven-proof serving bowl (2 cup capacity at least). Sprinkle with almonds.

2. Bake at 375° for 25 minutes or until bubbly and golden brown. Serve with dry toast points or crackers. Yield: 2 cups.

Artichoke Dip

1. Finely chop artichoke hearts in food processor or blender. Add other ingredients.

2. Heat at 250° in oven-proof serving dish until bubbly. Serve with crackers. Yield: 6 to 8 servings.

2 (8½ ounce) cans water-packed artichoke hearts, drained
1 cup mayonnaise
1 cup Parmesan cheese, grated
1 teaspoon dill weed
1 tablespoon instant minced onions

Chicken Liver Mold

1. Mince onion and saute in butter (reserving 3 tablespoons) until tender. Add chicken livers and cook about 10 minutes, stirring occasionally.

2. Add Marsala wine, spices, hot pepper sauce and garlic. Cook 5 minutes. Cool.

3. Heat chicken broth and soften gelatin in it. Pour ½ cup broth-gelatin mixture into a mold. Arrange sliced olives with pimento on bottom of mold; chill.

4. Place chicken livers, spices and Marsala in food processor or blender. Add bourbon and remaining chicken broth; blend until smooth.

5. Saute walnuts in 3 tablespoons butter until crisp; add to chicken liver mixture and pour into mold when gelatin in mold has set. Chill until firm.

6. Just before serving, invert mold onto serving plate. Garnish with lettuce or parsley. Serve with crackers or small bread slices. Yield: 10 to 12 servings.

1 onion
1 cup butter
¾ pound chicken livers
1½ cups chicken broth
2 tablespoons Marsala wine
½ teaspoon paprika
½ teaspoon allspice
½ teaspoon salt
   dash hot pepper sauce
1 clove garlic, minced
½ cup bourbon
½ cup chopped walnuts
1½ envelopes unflavored gelatin
   sliced green olives with pimento

California Guacamole

2 tablespoons sour cream
(or ranch-style dressing)
2 avocados, mashed
1 tablespoon lime juice
2 green onions, chopped
½ medium tomato,
chopped
2 tablespoons thick hot
picante sauce (or more
to taste)
¼ teaspoon garlic salt
Cheddar cheese, grated

1. Combine all of the ingredients, except the Cheddar cheese. Put in serving dish and top with cheese.

2. Serve with tortilla chips as a dip, or as an accompaniment to fajitas, tacos, enchiladas, etc. Yield: 4 to 6 servings.

Salinas Valley Vegetables with Confetti Dip

1 green pepper, finely
chopped
1 tomato, finely chopped
1 bunch green onions,
thinly sliced
½ cup sour cream
1 teaspoon dry mustard
1 teaspoon salt (optional)
½ teaspoon black pepper,
freshly ground
1 (8 ounce) package
cream cheese, softened

Assorted Fresh Vegetables:
caulifloweretts, broccoli
spears, celery stalks
and cherry tomatoes

1. Blend green pepper, tomato, onions, sour cream, mustard, salt, pepper and cream cheese together. Place in serving bowl, cover and chill for approximately 1 hour.

2. Serve with fresh vegetables for dipping. Can also be served with crackers. Yield: 6 to 8 servings.

Malaysian Peanut Dip

1. Mix ingredients until well blended.

2. Serve with raw vegetables such as jicama, pea pods, carrot sticks, bell pepper strips, cauliflower, celery sticks, or with pineapple spears or tofu puffs. Yield: 6 to 8 servings.

⅓ **cup crunchy peanut butter**
3 **tablespoons packed brown sugar**
½ **teaspoon red pepper flakes**
¼ **cup lemon juice**
2 **tablespoons cocktail sauce**
½ **cup soy sauce**

Veggie Dip

1. Mix all the ingredients except the sour cream. (Omit salt if serving with shrimp.) Fold in sour cream. Refrigerate until ready to use.

2. Serve with carrot and zucchini sticks, cherry tomatoes, cauliflower, and small wheat crackers for a colorful appetizer platter. Yield: 1½ cups.

1 **cup mayonnaise**
½ **tablespoon lemon juice**
¼ **teaspoon salt**
¼ **teaspoon paprika**
¼ **cup parsley, finely chopped**
1 **tablespoon grated onion**
1 **tablespoon chopped chives**
½ **teaspoon Worcestershire sauce**
1 **clove garlic, minced**
1 **tablespoon capers (optional)**
1 **(7 ounce) can shrimp (optional)**
½ **cup sour cream**

Curried Walnuts

4½ cups walnuts, bite-size, uniform pieces
1½ teaspoons salt
2½ teaspoons curry powder
2 tablespoons butter

1. Put nuts in boiling water for 1 to 2 minutes. Drain and put on jelly roll pan in a single layer. Bake at 350° for 20 minutes.

2. Melt butter, add salt and curry powder. Pour over nuts and stir well for uniform covering. Bake for an additional 5 minutes. Store in a closed jar.

3. Serve as an appetizer or chop and use in Waldorf salad, or sprinkled on tomato soup.

Salsa

1 bunch cilantro
4 medium jalapeno peppers
2 large carrots
2-3 stalks celery
1 large red onion
1 bunch green onions
2 bunches radishes
4-6 medium tomatoes
2 (1 pound 13 ounce) cans whole tomatoes
1 teaspoon salt
2 tablespoons sugar
2 tablespoons tamale spice
2 tablespoons medium chili powder
1 jigger red wine vinegar
1 jigger white wine vinegar
1 jigger tequila
1 tablespoon Mexican oregano

1. Using a steel blade in a food processor, chop the vegetables and place in a large bowl. Add the spices, vinegar and tequila while processing one of the following batches:

cilantro and jalapeno peppers — process fine

carrots, celery, red onion — process medium-fine

green onions and radishes — process medium-fine

fresh tomatoes — process medium

canned tomatoes, drained, juice reserved — process medium-fine

2. If necessary add additional juice from the tomatoes to thin.

Optional: Add one large bell pepper (red, green or yellow) chopped medium-fine.

Soups

SOUPS

For soup, the wine challenge is difficult. Your French onion soup or lobster bisque might require a weighty Cabernet Sauvignon to balance out the flavors. Experimentation with soups is a must.

Cold Avocado-Cream Soup

1. Peel avocado and cut into pieces. Puree in food processor or in blender. Add cucumber and process until smooth.

2. Add chicken broth and chives; blend.

3. Add lemon juice and sour cream; blend. Season with salt and pepper.

4. Chill and serve in soup bowls, garnished with sour cream and chives. Yield: 6 servings.

1 **large ripe avocado**
1 **large cucumber, peeled, seeded and cubed**
1½ **cups chicken broth**
2 **tablespoons finely chopped chives**
2 **tablespoons lemon juice**
¾ **cup sour cream**
salt and white pepper to taste

Garnish:
¼ **cup sour cream**
¼ **cup chopped chives**

Greek Lemon Soup

1. Combine chicken broth and rice in a 2½ quart saucepan. Bring to a boil, reduce heat. Cover and simmer for 15 to 20 minutes, or until rice is tender. Remove pan from heat.

2. Beat the eggs until fluffy and pale yellow, then beat in the lemon juice. Slowly pour about ⅓ of the soup mixture into the egg mixture (a drop at a time, to start), then whisk vigorously. Pour this mixture back into the rest of the soup, stirring vigorously. Soup should be slightly thickened.

3. Transfer soup to bowl and refrigerate until icy cold (5 hours or more).

4. Stir before serving. Garnish each serving with a lemon slice. Yield: 6 servings.

6 **cups chicken broth**
¼ **cup long-grain rice**
3 **eggs**
¼ **cup fresh lemon juice**
1 **lemon, sliced for garnish**

◊ Nutritional information per serving:

Calories 106	Fat .... 4 g	Iron .... 1 mg
Protein .... 9 g	Cholesterol .... 105 mg	Potassium .... 259 mg
Carbohydrates .... 8 g	Calcium .... 24 mg	Sodium .... 810 mg

Gazpacho

Soup Base and Spices:
- 1 **garlic clove, crushed**
- 1 **tablespoon sugar**
- 2 **teaspoons salt**
- 1 **(46 ounce) can tomato juice**
- 2 **tablespoons lemon juice**
- ½ **cup garlic oil (see note below) or ½ cup vegetable oil and 1 clove garlic, minced**
- 1 **teaspoon Worcestershire sauce**
- 1 **(7 ounce) can green chile salsa**
  hot pepper sauce to taste

Prepared Vegetables:
- 3 **tomatoes, finely diced**
- 1 **cucumber, peeled, seeded and finely diced**
- 1 **green pepper, finely diced**
- 2 **large carrots, shredded**
- 2 **large carrots, thinly sliced**
- ¼ **cup finely chopped onion**
- ¼ **cup thinly sliced celery**
- 1 **tablespoon chopped parsley**

1. Combine soup ingredients in large bowl; with electric mixer, blend on low speed. Chill.

2. Add prepared vegetables to bowl of liquid ingredients and chill thoroughly. Recipe is best if made a day ahead. Yield: 20 (½ cup) servings.

Optional: Add 1 pound cooked, cooled fresh shrimp.

Note: For garlic oil, place clove of garlic in ½ cup olive oil overnight. Remove garlic before using.

◊ Nutritional information per serving:

Calories 41	Fat ....4 g	Iron ....0.8 mg
Protein ....9 g	Cholesterol ....0 mg	Potassium ....318 mg
Carbohydrates ....9 g	Calcium ....29 mg	Sodium ....471 mg

White Gazpacho

1. Blend ingredients in blender. Chill.

2. Serve cold with colorful garnishes in separate dishes. Yield: 4 to 6 servings.

3 cucumbers, seeded, peeled and diced
2 cups chicken broth
2 cups sour cream
1 clove garlic, minced
2 tablespoons white vinegar
2 teaspoons salt

Garnishes:
sunflower seeds
chopped tomatoes
chopped green onions
black olives, sliced
dollops of sour cream

◊ Nutritional information per serving:

Calories	198	Fat	17 g	Iron	0.68 mg
Protein	5 g	Cholesterol	34 mg	Potassium	412 mg
Carbohydrates	8 g	Calcium	119 mg	Sodium	1013 mg

Lime and Tortilla Soup

1. Cut tortillas into 2½ inch strips. Pour oil ½ inch deep in small skillet. Fry tortillas in hot oil until browned and crisp; drain on paper towels.

2. Heat the 2 teaspoons oil in large saucepan, add onions and chiles; saute until onion is soft, but not browned. Add broth and chicken and bring to a boil. Cover and simmer for 20 minutes. Add tomato, simmer 5 minutes longer. Stir in lime juice.

3. To Serve: Ladle into bowls and add some fried tortilla strips. Float a lime slice in center of each serving. Yield: 4 servings.

2 corn tortillas
2 cups vegetable oil
2 teaspoons vegetable oil
⅓ cup onion, chopped
¼ cup canned green chiles, chopped
4 cups chicken broth
1 cup shredded, cooked chicken (1 whole chicken breast)
1 tomato, chopped
1 tablespoon lime juice
4 large lime slices

Pozole (Mexican Soup)

2 tablespoons vegetable oil

5 whole chicken breasts, skinned and cubed

2 medium onions, chopped

4 garlic cloves, minced

3 (14 ounce) cans yellow hominy

2 quarts water

4 beef or chicken bouillon cubes

2 tablespoons chili powder

1 tablespoon oregano leaves

1 teaspoon ground cumin

1 (28 ounce) can tomatoes

½ teaspoon pepper
salt to taste

2 pounds ham, cubed

Condiments:

1 cup sliced green onions

1 cup sliced radishes

1 small head lettuce, shredded

½ cup chopped cilantro

8 ounces Monterey Jack cheese, shredded
limes
salsa

1. In a large, 8 to 10 quart pan, heat oil over medium heat. Add chicken pieces and brown deeply. Set aside.

2. To the pan, add onion and garlic. Cook until onion is soft and transparent, stirring up browned bits on the bottom of pan.

3. Drain hominy, reserving liquid. Set hominy aside. To the pan, add hominy liquid, 2 quarts water, bouillon cubes, chili powder, oregano, cumin, tomatoes, pepper and ham. Bring to boiling; reduce heat, cover and simmer for 30 minutes. Add chicken pieces and continue simmering for 20 minutes. Stir in hominy and simmer 10 minutes longer, or until meats are tender. Skim off fat.

4. To serve: Ladle soup into warmed, wide soup bowls, allowing each bowl equal portions of chicken, ham and hominy. Place condiments in small bowls and allow guests to top soup with their choices. Yield: 8 to 10 servings.

Note: Soup can be made ahead. It freezes well. Can be doubled or halved.

Polish Soup

1. Rinse and sort lentils, or soak kidney beans. (Cover beans with water, bring to a boil and boil for 2 minutes. Remove from heat; cover and let stand for 1 hour. Drain beans, discard water.)

2. Combine all ingredients in large soup pot or crock pot. Cook 2½ hours (or until beans are tender) over low heat, or overnight in crock pot.

3. Serve with dollop of sour cream, if desired. Yield: 10 to 12 servings.

1   cup dry kidney beans or lentils
12-16 ounces Polish sausage, cut into 1 inch slices
1   small cabbage, sliced
1   medium onion, chopped
3   carrots, chopped
1   (15 ounce) can tomatoes
1   (6 ounce) can tomato sauce
3   cups water
      salt and pepper to taste

Note: The Polish sausage may be simmered in water to remove some of the fat before adding to the soup pot. Or follow above instructions and then chill soup, skim fat off top and re-heat.

Minestrone Soup

1. In a large pot, combine water, beans, oxtail, bouillon cubes, Italian seasoning, salt and garlic. Cover and simmer until beans are tender (about 2 hours).

2. Add carrots, potatoes, onion, celery and stewed tomatoes. Cover and bring to a boil; reduce heat and simmer for ½ hour. Then add the macaroni and cabbage. Bring to a boil again and simmer for another ½ hour.

3. Remove oxtails and take off the meat; shred and return to soup. Add additional salt to taste. Yield: 10 to 12 servings.

4   quarts water
1   cup pink or pinto beans
1   cup lentils
2   pounds beef oxtails
6   beef bouillon cubes
1½   teaspoons Italian seasoning
1   teaspoon salt
1   garlic clove, minced
2   carrots, sliced
3   potatoes, diced
1   onion, sliced
3   celery stalks, sliced
2   (1 pound) cans stewed tomatoes, Italian style, chopped
2   cups small pasta shells or macaroni
4   cups shredded cabbage

Note: If you wish you may cook the beans, lentils, beef with the seasonings ahead. Let cool in the refrigerator overnight and skim the fat. Then add the remaining ingredients and cook as noted.

Zucchini Minestre

2 stalks celery, chopped
2 carrots, chopped
1 onion, chopped
1-2 cloves garlic, minced
½ cup chopped parsley
4 zucchini, chopped
2 tablespoons olive oil
2 tablespoons butter
    seasoned salt and
    pepper
4-6 cups chicken broth
1 cup chopped fresh
    tomatoes or 1 (14
    ounce) can tomatoes
½ pound spaghetti, broken
    in half
    grated Parmesan
    cheese
    dried red pepper flakes
    (optional)

1. Saute celery, carrots, onion, garlic and parsley in olive oil and butter until soft. Add zucchini and cook until tender-crisp. Season with seasoned salt and pepper.

2. Add chicken broth and bring to a boil. Add tomatoes and pasta; cook, stirring frequently, until pasta is tender.

3. Serve with fresh grated Parmesan cheese and dried red pepper flakes (optional). Yield: 4 to 6 servings.

◊ Nutritional information per serving:

Calories 281	Fat .... 10 g	Iron .... 3 mg
Protein .... 11 g	Cholesterol .... 11 mg	Potassium .... 682 mg
Carbohydrates .... 37 g	Calcium .... 54 mg	Sodium .... 713 mg

Ham and Barley Soup

¼ cup butter
¼ cup finely chopped
    onion
1 cup pearl barley
5½ cups chicken broth
¼ pound baked ham, cut
    into thin strips
¼ teaspoon pepper
1 cup heavy cream
1 small can peas
1 cup grated Parmesan
    cheese (optional)
    grated nutmeg (optional)

1. In a 5 to 6 quart Dutch oven, stir butter and onions over medium heat and cook until onions are soft, about 5 minutes. Add barley and cook and stir until golden.

2. Stir in broth, ham and pepper. Bring to a boil; cover and simmer until barley is tender, about 30 minutes. Add cream and peas. Cook until just thoroughly heated.

3. Pour into bowls and garnish with Parmesan cheese and nutmeg if desired. Yield: 4 to 6 servings.

Italian Sausage Soup

1. In a 5 quart pot, cook the sausages over medium heat until lightly browned. Drain off and discard any fat. Add the garlic and onions and cook, stirring, until soft.

2. Add tomatoes (including liquid). Using a spoon, break tomatoes into pieces. Add the beef broth, wine or water, and the basil. Simmer, uncovered, for 30 minutes.

3. Chill, then later remove fat and discard.

4. Add parsley, green pepper, zucchini and pasta; simmer, covered, for 25 minutes. Serve immediately. Ladle into bowls and pass grated Parmesan cheese to sprinkle over individual servings. Yield: 6 servings.

1½ pounds mild Italian sausage, cut into ½ inch lengths
2 cloves garlic, minced
2 large onions, chopped
1 (28 ounce) can Italian-style, pear-shaped tomatoes
5 cups beef broth
1½ cups dry red wine or water
4 tablespoons fresh chopped basil
3 tablespoons fresh chopped parsley
1 medium green pepper, chopped
2 medium zucchini, sliced ¼ inch thick
3 cups uncooked bow-tie pasta
  freshly grated Parmesan cheese

Creamy Carrot-Dill Soup

1. Melt butter in saucepan and add onions; cook until soft.

2. Add carrots, salt and pepper and chicken broth. Cook over low heat 30 minutes, or until carrots are tender.

3. Puree in food processor until smooth. Add ricotta and blend until smooth. Put back in saucepan and heat. Add wine and dill. Yield: 4 to 6 servings.

2 tablespoons butter
1 cup finely chopped onion
5 cups sliced carrots (1½ pounds)
½ teaspoon salt
  pepper to taste
4 cups chicken broth
¼ cup ricotta cheese
2 tablespoons port wine
2 tablespoons fresh dill or 1 tablespoon dry dill

◊ Nutritional information per serving:

Calories	144	Fat	6 g	Iron	1 mg
Protein	6 g	Cholesterol	16 mg	Potassium	583 mg
Carbohydrates	15 g	Calcium	75 mg	Sodium	777 mg

Cream of Asparagus Soup

3-4 pounds asparagus
3 tablespoons unsalted butter
½ yellow onion, chopped
1 clove garlic, minced
⅛ cup chopped basil
3 tablespoons flour
6 cups chicken broth
1 cup heavy cream (can substitute half and half) salt and pepper to taste

1. Steam asparagus, cut into 2 inch slices, reserving the tips.

2. Saute onion in butter for 5 minutes over medium heat. Add the garlic and basil and continue cooking until garlic is tender. Add flour and ½ cup broth, making a roux. Add remaining broth and bring to a boil. Add tender asparagus (reserving tips). Simmer approximately one hour.

3. Blend soup in food processor. Return to soup pot, add cream and heat thoroughly. Place in individual bowls and garnish with reserved asparagus tips. Yield: 8 to 10 servings.

Cream of Zucchini Soup

4 tablespoons chopped scallions (including green tops)
2 garlic cloves, minced
2 pounds zucchini, sliced thin
4 tablespoons butter
1 tablespoon curry (or to taste)
1 teaspoon salt
1 cup heavy cream
4 cups chicken broth

1. In a tightly covered pan, simmer onion, garlic and zucchini in butter until barely tender, about 10 minutes. Stir often to prevent burning.

2. Put the mixture in a food processor with enough broth to blend until smooth. Put back in soup pan and add the rest of the broth, cream, curry and salt. Simmer until just hot enough to serve. It can be refrigerated at this point to be served cold. Yield: 4 to 6 servings.

Note: If freezing soup, omit cream until serving time. This soup can also be made in the microwave oven — simmer for 5 minutes before blending in the food processor.

Cream of Cauliflower Soup

1. Heat oil in 8 to 10 quart pot, add onion and saute over medium heat. Add carrot and celery and cook, stirring frequently. Add cauliflower and 1 tablespoon parsley. Cover, reduce heat to low and cook 15 minutes, stirring occasionally to prevent mixture from sticking.

2. Add chicken stock and bouquet garni and bring to a boil over medium-high heat. Reduce heat and simmer for about 5 minutes.

3. Melt butter in 2 quart saucepan; remove from heat. Stir in flour and slowly add milk and half-and-half. Bring to a boil, stirring constantly until it is thick and smooth.

4. Slowly stir butter-milk mixture into simmering soup. Season with salt and pepper to taste. If soup is too thick, add more chicken broth. Garnish with sprinkling of paprika. Yield: 6 servings.

2 **tablespoons vegetable oil**
½ **cup chopped onion**
1 **carrot, grated**
1 **cup chopped celery**
1 **pound cauliflower, cut into flowerets**
2 **tablespoons chopped parsley**
5 **cups chicken broth**
1 **bouquet garni (place ½ teaspoon peppercorns, 1 teaspoon tarragon, and ½ bay leaf in a cheesecloth square; bring corners together and tie)**
¼ **cup butter**
¾ **cup flour**
2 **cups milk**
1 **cup half-and-half paprika salt and pepper to taste**

French Onion Soup

6 **large onions, sliced**
3 **tablespoons butter**
1 **tablespoon sugar**
6 **cups boiling water**
12 **cubes beef bouillon**
salt and pepper to taste
nutmeg to taste
½ **cup white wine**
6 **pieces dry French bread**
6 **whole slices Swiss**
cheese, halved

1. Brown onions in butter until soft. Add 1 tablespoon sugar to make it brown faster.

2. Dissolve bouillon cubes in 1 cup water and add to onions. Add remaining 5 cups of water. Sprinkle salt and pepper to taste. Add nutmeg. Simmer, covered, for 30 minutes. Add wine, heat through.

3. Pour into individual crockery soup bowls. Place a slice of French bread on top. Carefully place two slices of Swiss cheese on top of the crock, overlapping the edges. Place the crocks on a cookie sheet. Broil 4 inches from heat, until brown and bubbly. Serve. Yield: 6 servings.

Green Pea Soup

2 **cups chicken broth**
1 **medium carrot, finely**
diced
1 **teaspoon chervil leaves**
1½ **cups fresh peas or 1 (10**
ounce) package frozen
peas, thawed
2 **tablespoons butter**
salt and pepper to taste

1. In a heavy 2½ to 3 quart saucepan, bring chicken broth, carrot and chervil to a boil. Reduce heat and simmer, covered, for 10 to 15 minutes or until carrots are tender. Remove from heat and add peas.

2. Place half the mixture in a blender or food processor and blend until smooth. Repeat with second half of mixture. Return to pan and stir in butter. Heat thoroughly and serve. Yield: 4 to 5 servings.

◊ Nutritional information per serving:

Calories 98	Fat .... 5 g	Iron .... 0.93 mg
Protein .... 5 g	Cholesterol .... 13 g	Potassium .... 239 mg
Carbohydrates .... 8 g	Calcium .... 20 mg	Sodium .... 356 mg

Potato Soup

1. Brown bacon until crisp. Drain and reserve approximately ¼ cup bacon drippings. Cook onion in drippings on medium heat until soft and translucent.

2. Add potatoes and chicken broth. Bring to a boil and simmer until potatoes are soft, about 15 minutes. Add light cream and seasonings and heat (do not boil). Add reserved bacon and serve. Yield: 4 to 6 servings.

6-8 slices thick sliced bacon, chopped
1 large onion, sliced and halved
6 medium potatoes, pared and diced
4 cups chicken broth
2 cups light cream
6 tablespoons chopped fresh parsley
2 teaspoons or more hot pepper sauce
salt and pepper to taste

Wine/Broccoli/Cheese Soup

1. In a large soup pot, cook broccoli in chicken stock and bay leaf until tender, about 20 minutes.

2. Meanwhile, saute onions in butter until transparent. Remove from heat and add flour. Mix well. When broccoli is tender, remove bay leaf and puree in blender with chicken stock. Return to pot; add onion mixture, parsley, thyme, sage, nutmeg, pepper, and Worcestershire sauce. Stir until thoroughly blended. Heat on low heat.

3. Mix egg yolk with cream and one cup of the soup. Return to the pot along with the cheese and wine. Stir to blend. Heat thoroughly and serve, garnished with fresh parsley. Yield: 6 servings.

1 pound broccoli
2 cups chicken stock
1 bay leaf
¼ cup chopped onion
2 tablespoons butter
1 tablespoon flour
2 tablespoons chopped parsley
¼ teaspoon dried thyme
¼ teaspoon dried sage
pinch of nutmeg
¼ teaspoon ground pepper
dash Worcestershire sauce
1 egg yolk
½ cup heavy cream
1 cup sharp Cheddar cheese
¼ cup good Sauterne wine
fresh parsley

Dramatic Two-Soup Combination

Sweet Pea Soup:

- 6 **tablespoons unsalted butter**
- 1 **large yellow onion, coarsely chopped**
- 3 **cloves garlic, peeled and chopped**
- 4 **cups chicken broth (preferably homemade)**
- 1 **large potato, peeled and quartered**
- 1½ **pounds frozen sweet peas**
- ¼ **teaspoon cayenne pepper**
- ½ **teaspoon freshly ground black pepper**
- 2 **tablespoons thyme, crumbled**

1. In a heavy saucepan over low heat, place butter, onion and garlic and cook until wilted, about 10 minutes.

2. Add chicken broth and potato; bring to a boil. Reduce heat and cook about 15 minutes, until potato is tender.

3. Add peas, cayenne and black pepper and return to boil. Remove from heat and stir in thyme. Let sit for 10 minutes.

4. In a food processor fitted with steel blade, or in a blender, process soup in small batches until smooth.

Sweet Pepper Soup:

- 4 **medium red bell peppers, cored, seeded and cut into strips**
- 20 **ripe Italian plum tomatoes, quartered**
- ⅓ **cup fresh lemon juice**
- 1 **teaspoon ground ginger**
- ½ **teaspoon freshly ground black pepper**

1. In a heavy saucepan over low heat, combine all ingredients. Cover and simmer for 30 minutes, until peppers are tender. Stir occasionally. Remove from heat.

2. In a food processor fitted with a steel blade or in a blender, puree the mixture until smooth.

To Assemble the Soup for Presentation:

- **sour cream or creme fraiche**
- **chopped fresh basil**

1. Heat both soups in separate pans.

2. Have heated shallow soup bowls ready. At the same time, pour ½ cup of the Sweet Pea Soup and ½ cup of the Sweet Pepper Soup from either side of each bowl. Each color soup will retain its own identity. Garnish each bowl with a dollop of sour cream or creme fraiche (available in

specialty stores) and a sprinkling of chopped fresh basil. Yield: 6 servings.

◊ Nutritional information per serving:

Calories 245	Fat .... 11 g	Iron .... 5 mg
Protein .... 10 g	Cholesterol .... 24 mg	Potassium .... 933 mg
Carbohydrates .... 31 g	Calcium .... 72 mg	Sodium .... 581 mg

Zucchini Soup

1. Boil zucchini, onion, chicken broth and seasonings in 4 quart saucepan over medium high heat until zucchini is very tender.

2. Carefully blend warm soup in food processor or blender, including bacon pieces, until smooth.

3. Serve with Parmesan cheese on top. Yield: 8 servings.

3 pounds zucchini, cut in large pieces
1 large onion, chopped
4 cups chicken broth
½ teaspoon salt
4 tablespoons fresh chopped basil
pepper to taste
4 slices bacon, cooked to crisp, crumbled
grated Parmesan cheese

◊ Nutritional information per serving:

Calories 86	Fat .... 4 g	Iron .... 3 mg
Protein .... 7 g	Cholesterol .... 6 mg	Potassium .... 630 mg
Carbohydrates .... 7 g	Calcium .... 130 mg	Sodium .... 643 mg

Crab-Vegetable Bisque

½ **cup butter**
2 **tablespoons chopped onion**
¼ **cup flour**
4 **cups milk**
2 **teaspoons chicken bouillon granules**
1 **teaspoon salt**
½ **teaspoon pepper**
2 **teaspoons chopped parsley**
½ **teaspoon grated nutmeg**
½ **pound fresh Dungeness or Snow crab meat (reserve some nice pieces for garnish)**
½ **pound broccoli and cauliflower, chopped**

1. Melt butter in a 4½ quart Dutch oven over medium-low heat. Add onions and cook slowly, 5 to 8 minutes, until softened. Add flour and stir to blend. Cook, stirring, about 3 minutes. Add milk slowly while stirring and blend well. Add parsley and spices and bring to a boil over increased heat. Reduce heat and simmer until mixture begins to thicken, about 10 minutes.

2. Add crab and vegetables and cook until vegetables are tender-crisp and soup is creamy, about 10 to 15 minutes. Garnish with reserved crab meat and chopped parsley. Yield: 4 to 6 servings.

Salads

SALADS AND DRESSINGS

Wine is usually a poor match for salads, because the vinegar in most salad dressings tends to kill the taste buds for the impact of the wine. You can enjoy a light red wine with a creamy cheese-based dressing.

California Artichoke Salad

1. Trim artichokes by removing coarse outer leaves and cutting stem even with base so that they will stand upright. With a sharp knife, cut off the top third of each artichoke and trim thorns from remaining leaves. Bring 4 quarts of water and vinegar to boiling. Add artichokes, cover and simmer gently until stem ends pierce readily with a fork, about 30 minutes.

2. Drain and let artichokes cool slightly, then remove thistle from center with a spoon. Drizzle cavities, tips and base with lemon juice. Cool, wrap and refrigerate for one hour, or until the next day.

3. Combine tomato, bacon, rice, green onion, peas and parsley. Stir in ½ cup of the Herb Mayonnaise Dressing. Spoon vegetable mixture into artichokes and serve remaining sauce for dipping leaves. Yield: 6 servings.

6 **large artichokes**
2 **tablespoons vinegar**
2 **tablespoons lemon juice**
8 **strips bacon, cooked, drained and crumbled**
1 **small meaty tomato, seeded and diced**
1 **cup cold cooked rice**
⅓ **cup sliced green onions**
½ **cup frozen peas, thawed**
2 **tablespoons chopped parsley**

Herb Mayonnaise Dressing:
½ **cup olive oil**
2 **tablespoons white wine vinegar**
2 **tablespoons chopped fresh basil or ¼ teaspoon dried basil**
¼ **teaspoon dried oregano**
¼ **teaspoon garlic powder**
¼ **teaspoon paprika**
1 **cup mayonnaise**

Overnight Cauliflower Salad

1. Toss together lettuce, cauliflower, onion and sugar and place in large salad bowl.

2. Top with bacon and spread mayonnaise over the top, sealing the edges. Top with cheese and cover tightly with plastic wrap. Chill overnight. Yield: 8 to 10 servings.

1 **large head iceberg lettuce, broken into small pieces**
1 **large head cauliflower, broken into bite-sized pieces**
2 **tablespoons minced green onion**
2 **tablespoons sugar**
1 **pound bacon, cooked and crumbled**
1½ **cups mayonnaise**
½ **cup grated Swiss cheese**

Artichokes Vinaigrette

4 medium artichokes
1 lemon, juice only (about 2 tablespoons)

Vinaigrette Dressing:
¾ cup olive oil
⅓ cup balsamic vinegar
1 tablespoon Dijon mustard
¼ teaspoon salt
½ teaspoon dried dill

1. Trim artichokes by removing coarse outer leaves and cutting stem even with base so that they will stand upright. With a sharp knife, cut off the top third of each artichoke and trim thorns from remaining leaves.

2. Steam artichokes over several inches of simmering water, to which juice of ½ lemon has been added, about 30 minutes. When tender, remove from pan and cool, inverted on rack.

3. Carefully spread apart leaves and remove thistle from the center of the artichoke. Chill, covered.

4. Whisk together oil, vinegar, mustard, salt and dill. Chill. Just before serving, put about ¼ cup of dressing inside each artichoke and serve on individual serving plates. Yield: 4 servings.

Artichoke and Shrimp Salad

2 pounds medium shrimp, shelled and deveined
2 cups broccoli flowerets
2 (8 ounce) jars marinated artichoke hearts
2 cups cherry tomatoes
8-10 scallions, cut into ¾ inch pieces, green part included
2 cups mayonnaise
1 heaping tablespoon Dijon mustard

1. Cook shrimp in boiling water for 1 minute. Drain and cool.

2. Cook broccoli in boiling water 3 to 5 minutes. Put immediately in ice water to stop cooking.

3. Cut artichokes into bite-sized pieces. Combine artichokes and marinade with shrimp, broccoli, tomatoes and onions in mixing bowl.

4. Mix Dijon mustard with mayonnaise. Toss with salad to coat well. Cover and refrigerate until ready to serve. Yield: 6 to 8 servings.

Optional: Use 1 pound of shrimp and add ½ pound cooked pasta shells or fusilli (corkscrews).

Broccoli-Artichoke Cashew Salad

1. Parboil broccoli for 5 minutes, remove from pan, drain and cool slightly, then dice. Tear lettuce into bite-sized pieces.

2. Combine all vegetables and the cashews in a large bowl.

3. Mix together dressing ingredients in a blender or food processor. Toss with vegetables in bowl, serve immediately. Yield: 10 servings.

1 bunch broccoli
1 head butter lettuce
1 red onion, diced
2 cucumbers, sliced
2 (8½ ounce) cans arti-
 choke hearts, drained
 (not marinated)
6 ounces frozen peas,
 thawed
3-4 ounces cashews

Dressing:
 ½ cup olive oil
 2 tablespoons balsamic or
 red wine vinegar
 1 teaspoon anchovy paste
 (optional)
1-2 tablespoons chopped
 parsley
 1 small clove garlic,
 minced
 salt and pepper to taste

Fresh Broccoli Salad

1. Toss together broccoli, raisins, red onion and bacon in a large bowl.

2. Prepare dressing by mixing mayonnaise, sugar, vinegar and pepper. Mix with salad ingredients and refrigerate, covered, for at least two hours.

3. Toss with sunflower seeds just before serving. Yield: 10 to 12 servings.

2 pounds fresh broccoli
 flowerets
½ cup raisins
⅓ cup finely chopped red
 onion
6 slices cooked, crisp
 bacon, crumbled
½ cup sunflower seeds

Dressing:
 1 cup mayonnaise
 ¼ cup sugar
 2 tablespoons vinegar
 fresh ground pepper

Optional: Add one cup chopped peanuts.

Broccoli-Cauliflower Salad

1 head cauliflowerets
1 head broccoli flowerets
1 red onion, sliced in rings
   or 3 green onions, sliced
½-1 cup halved seedless red
   grapes

Dressing:
1 cup mayonnaise
½ cup sour cream
1 tablespoon sugar
1 tablespoon vinegar
   dash of Worcestershire
   sauce
   dash of hot pepper
   sauce
   salt and pepper to taste

1. Place onion slices in a bowl and cover with boiling water. Let set for 30 minutes, then drain.

2. Combine all vegetables and the grapes in a bowl. Mix dressing ingredients together and mix with vegetables. Cover and chill. Yield: 8 to 10 servings.

Optional: Add grated carrots and/or chopped olives for a more colorful appearance.

Zucchini Salad

4 zucchini, sliced thinly
1 head cauliflower, broken
   into bite-sized pieces
1 medium red onion,
   sliced
1 (6 ounce) can black
   olives, pitted

Dressing:
¾ cup vegetable oil
½ cup wine vinegar
1-2 tablespoons sugar
1 teaspoon salt
1 teaspoon celery seeds
1 teaspoon dry mustard

1. Cover red onion slices with boiling water and let sit for 30 minutes. Drain.

2. Mix zucchini, cauliflower, onion and olives together in bowl. Blend dressing ingredients well and add to salad. Toss well.

3. Marinate overnight, covered, in refrigerator. Yield: 8 to 10 servings.

◊ Nutritional information per serving:

Calories 213	Fat .... 20 g	Iron .... 1 mg
Protein .... 3 g	Cholesterol .... 0 mg	Potassium .... 464 mg
Carbohydrates .... 9 g	Calcium .... 59 mg	Sodium .... 363 mg

Eggplant Salad

1. Leaving the skin on, slice each eggplant lengthwise in half, then each half into 4 lengthwise pieces. Spread the 24 long slices on cookie sheets and sprinkle liberally with salt. Let stand 30 to 45 minutes until the slices "sweat". Blot moisture with paper towels.

2. Brush eggplant with a little of the olive oil and brown on both sides in a frying pan until lightly brown.

3. Saute onions and green peppers in olive oil. When onions are soft, add tomatoes, parsley, salt and pepper. Cook for 3 minutes over medium heat.

4. Arrange slices of eggplant in a very large shallow baking dish, one layer deep only. Pack eggplant tight as they shrink up and you want the sauce to stay on top. Spread with onion, pepper and tomato mixture. If too dry, add a little water. Bake for 45 minutes at 300°. Remove from oven and add wine vinegar.

5. Refrigerate, covered, until serving time. Serve cold or bring to room temperature before serving. Yield: 8 to 10 servings.

3 large eggplants
1 cup olive oil
1½ pounds onions, chopped
½ pound green pepper, chopped
1 cup chopped parsley
1 (20 ounce) can solid pack tomatoes
¼ cup wine vinegar
salt and pepper to taste

Note: A wonderful accompaniment to lamb dishes.

◊ Nutritional information per serving:

Calories 297	Fat .... 22 g	Iron .... 3 mg
Protein .... 4 g	Cholesterol .... 0 mg	Potassium .... 886 mg
Carbohydrates .... 25 g	Calcium .... 130 mg	Sodium .... 197 mg

Tomato, Fennel, Parmigiano Salad

6 **Roma tomatoes, sliced**
1 **bulb fennel, sliced lengthwise**
2 **heads Belgian endive, sliced crosswise**
shaved imported Parmigiano cheese, to taste
salt and pepper to taste
olive oil
balsamic vinegar
fresh chopped basil, for garnish
lime slices, for garnish

1. Arrange tomatoes, fennel and endive in serving bowl. Cover with shaved Parmigiano cheese and salt and pepper to taste.

2. Drizzle with olive oil, then balsamic vinegar. Garnish with fresh chopped basil and fresh lime slices. Yield: 6 servings.

Cobb Salad

1 **medium head iceberg lettuce, shredded**
1 **medium avocado, sliced or diced**
3 **cups cooked, shredded chicken breast**
½ **pound bacon, cooked crisp and crumbled**
2 **large tomatoes, diced**
2 **hard-boiled eggs, grated**
½ **cup crumbled bleu cheese**

Dressing:
½ **cup vegetable oil**
¼ **cup white vinegar**
1 **teaspoon salt**
2 **teaspoons sugar (optional)**
¾ **teaspoon pepper**
1¼ **teaspoons dry mustard**
1 **clove garlic, minced**
⅓ **cup chopped fresh parsley**

1. Place all ingredients except dressing in a large bowl.

2. Mix together dressing ingredients. Pour over lettuce and chicken mixture. Toss to coat with dressing and serve immediately. Yield: 8 servings.

Peas with Bacon and Sour Cream

1. Mix together the peas, onions, celery, salt and pepper and sour cream. Just before serving, add the bacon and cashews. Yield: 6 servings.

1 **(16 ounce) package thawed, frozen peas**
⅓ **cup chopped green onions**
1 **cup chopped celery salt and pepper to taste**
1 **cup sour cream**
⅓ **cup bacon, fried crisp and crumbled**
⅓ **cup cashews, coarsely cut**

Corn Salad

1. Mix all ingredients together in a large bowl, with the exception of the green olives. Cover and refrigerate 3 hours or overnight.

2. Before serving, garnish with green olive slices and serve with a slotted spoon. Yield: 6 to 8 servings.

4 **cups fresh or frozen cooked corn**
1 **(2 ounce) jar chopped pimentos**
½ **cup finely chopped green onions**
2 **ribs celery, finely chopped**
¼ **cup sugar**
½ **cup vegetable oil**
½ **cup white vinegar**
½ **teaspoon salt**
½ **teaspoon pepper**
4 **pimento-stuffed green olives for garnish (optional)**

◊ Nutritional information per serving:

Calories 222	Fat .... 15 g	Iron .... 0.76 mg
Protein .... 3 g	Cholesterol .... 0 mg	Potassium .... 270 mg
Carbohydrates .... 23 g	Calcium .... 12 mg	Sodium .... 201 mg

Fresh Corn and Red Pepper Salad

10-12 ears of white corn
4 tablespoons butter
1 clove garlic, minced
1 bunch green onions,
chopped
1 large red pepper,
chopped
¼ cup water
salt and pepper
½ cup chopped fresh basil
2 tablespoons lime juice
1 head radicchio, sepa-
rated into leaves (can
substitute red leaf
lettuce)
lime wedges for garnish

1. Clean corn kernels from ears of corn with a sharp knife. Set aside. Saute 2 tablespoons of the butter with garlic, chopped red pepper and chopped green onion for 2 minutes.

2. Add corn and water and cook on high heat for 2 to 3 minutes, or until water has evaporated. Add the 2 remaining tablespoons of butter, salt and pepper, basil, lime juice and mix well.

3. Spoon into radicchio leaves for individual servings, garnish with lime wedges. Yield: 6 to 8 servings.

◊ Nutritional information per serving:

Calories 168	Fat .... 7 g	Iron .... 2 mg
Protein .... 5 g	Cholesterol .... 16 mg	Potassium .... 540 mg
Carbohydrates .... 26 g	Calcium .... 71 mg	Sodium .... 72 mg

Caesar Salad

1. Crush garlic in a small bowl and add oil. Let stand several hours.

2. Place 2 tablespoons of the garlic oil in a skillet over medium heat. Add bread cubes and toast until lightly browned, stirring often. (Or, coat bread with oil and toast in 325° oven.)

3. Place the lettuce in a large salad bowl and season with salt and pepper, Worcestershire sauce and dry mustard. Add the remaining ¼ cup garlic oil and mix until every leaf is glossy.

4. Coddle the egg in hot water for 1 minute exactly. Break the egg into the salad and squeeze the lemon juice and mix thoroughly. Add the chopped anchovies and Parmesan and mix again. Lastly, add the French bread croutons and mix gently. Taste for seasoning. Serve immediately. Yield: 6 servings.

1 **small clove garlic, crushed**
6 **tablespoons olive oil**
1 **cup dry French bread cubes (½ inch cubes)**
1 **large head romaine, washed and torn into bite-sized pieces**
¼ **teaspoon salt freshly ground pepper**
1 **egg**
1 **lemon, juice only (more according to taste) dash Worcestershire sauce**
¼ **teaspoon dry mustard**
3-4 **anchovy fillets**
¼ **cup freshly grated Parmesan cheese**

Chinese Chicken Noodle Salad

6 pounds chicken breasts, boned and skinned
½ cup hoisin sauce
¼ cup oyster sauce
6 tablespoons peanut oil
2 tablespoons chile paste with garlic
¼ cup soy sauce
¼ cup honey
2 pounds oriental noodles
3 tablespoons peanut oil
4 red or yellow peppers, cut into strips, then sliced diagonally
3 pounds thin asparagus, cut diagonally in 1 inch pieces, steamed crispy tender
1 bunch green onions, tops included, cut on diagonal
1 pound Chinese pea pods, very lightly steamed
1 cup slivered almonds, toasted
OPTIONAL: other vegetables may be added or substituted

1. In a large roasting pan, combine the hoisin sauce, oyster sauce, peanut oil, chile paste, soy sauce and honey. Marinate the chicken breasts for at least 1 hour. Bake in marinade at 400° for 25 to 30 minutes, or just until tender. When cool enough to handle, cut into strips and set aside.

2. Cook oriental noodles, drain and toss with 3 tablespoons peanut oil. Prepare vegetables. Whisk together the dressing ingredients in a large bowl.

3. Place on decorative platter or shallow bowl and arrange vegetables in the center. Serve with extra dressing on the side. Yield: 24 servings.

Dressing:
3 cloves garlic
2 tablespoons fresh ginger, grated
½ cup balsamic vinegar
¼ cup honey
2 cups soy sauce
¾ cup sesame oil
3 tablespoons chile oil

Note: The chicken, Chinese noodles, vegetables and dressing can all be made ahead of time. When ready to serve, toss chicken, noodles and enough dressing to coat well together and mix well.

Chicken Salad with Curry-Chutney Dressing

1. Combine chicken with green pepper, scallions, celery, grapes and cantaloupe.

2. Mix together dressing ingredients and toss with chicken mixture. Serve on a bed of lettuce garnished with bunches of grapes, or stuffed in tomatoes, papayas or avocado halves. Yield: 10 to 12 servings.

4 pounds chicken, cooked and diced
1 cup chopped green pepper
1 cup minced scallions
2 cups chopped celery
2 cups red seedless grapes
1 cup diced cantaloupe

Dressing:
1¼ cups mayonnaise
¾ cup plain yogurt
1 tablespoon curry powder
⅓ cup chutney

Pea Pod and Chicken Salad

1. Combine dressing ingredients in a jar. Shake well and chill.

2. Combine chicken, pea pods, spinach, nectarines and walnuts in a medium bowl. Pour half of the chilled dressing on top and toss to coat well. Add more dressing to taste. Serve immediately. Yield: 6 to 8 servings.

3 cups cooked, cubed chicken
½ pound fresh pea pods, lightly steamed until tender-crisp
5 cups torn fresh spinach
6 nectarines, thinly sliced
½ cup walnut pieces

Dressing:
½ cup vegetable oil
½ cup vinegar
2 tablespoons dry sherry
2 tablespoons soy sauce
2 teaspoons sugar

◊ Nutritional information per serving:

Calories 260	Fat............................14 g	Iron ....3 mg
Protein ....19 g	Cholesterol ....40 mg	Potassium ....575 mg
Carbohydrates ....16 g	Calcium ....65 mg	Sodium ....193 mg

Oriental Chicken Salad in Lettuce Bundles

Sauce:
- ½ **teaspoon salt**
- ½ **teaspoon dry mustard**
- 1 **teaspoon chicken bouillon granules**
- 1½ **teaspoons cornstarch**
- 1-2 **teaspoons chile powder (depending on taste)**
- ½ **cup hot water**
- 1½ **teaspoons minced ginger root**
- ¾ **teaspoon minced garlic**

Chicken Salad:
- 1½ **pounds boneless chicken breasts, skinned and diced in ¼ inch cubes**
- 3 **tablespoons soy sauce**
- 2 **tablespoons peanut oil**
- 1 **(8 ounce) can water chestnuts, finely chopped**
- 1 **cup finely chopped celery**
- ½ **cup finely chopped scallions**
- 1 **cup finely chopped mushrooms**
- 2 **heads Boston lettuce, separated but left in large leaves, rinsed, drained and chilled slivers of almonds (optional)**
- ¼ **package maifun (dried rice threads, found in Oriental section of supermarket or specialty store ... saifun can be substituted)**

1. In a small bowl, mix together the salt, mustard, chicken bouillon granules, cornstarch and chile powder. Stir in hot water and stir until smooth. Add ginger root and garlic. Set aside.

2. Mix chicken with soy sauce and let stand for 15 minutes. In a 10 inch skillet, heat the oil and add the chicken mixture. Stir-fry fast for a few minutes. Add the sauce mixture, stirring constantly. Cook over high heat until sauce thickens and excess liquid is reduced. Chicken and vegetables should have only a light coating of the thick sauce to bind them together.

3. In a medium-sized saucepan, heat 2 inches of vegetable oil. When it is hot, break a little portion of maifun off and put it in hot oil and brown lightly. (Oil should be hot but not over 380° or the maifun will brown but not puff.) The maifun expands when it is put into hot oil, so be careful not to put too much in at once. Drain on paper towels. You will only need a small portion of the package for this dish, less than ¼ of a package.

4. To serve: Spread the maifun to cover the platter. Put the chicken mixture on top and sprinkle with almonds. Put the lettuce on another platter or bowl. Pass lettuce, then chicken mixture. Each person places the lettuce on their plate, puts a small portion of the chicken-maifun mixture in the middle and wraps the lettuce around it to eat. Yield: 3¼ to 4 cups dressing; 6 servings salad.

◊ Nutritional information per serving:
Calories 289   Fat .... 10 g   Iron .... 4 mg
Protein .... 36 g   Cholesterol .... 87 mg   Potassium .... 798 mg
Carbohydrates .... 14 g   Calcium .... 137 mg   Sodium .... 877 mg

Antipasto Salad

1. Combine the tuna, Giardiniera, green and black olives, onions and mushrooms in a large bowl.

2. Add artichoke hearts and marinade, tomato sauce, vinegar, oil, salt and pepper. Toss all ingredients lightly. Let stand 24 hours in the refrigerator before serving. Yield: 8 to 10 servings.

1 (6 ounce) can water packed tuna, drained
1 (16 ounce) jar Giardiniera (assorted vegetables in vinegar — not hot)
1 (10 ounce) jar green olives, Spanish style, drained
1 (6 ounce) can pitted black olives, drained
1 (7½ ounce) jar small white onions
1 (4 ounce) can button mushrooms, drained
1 (6 ounce) jar marinated artichoke hearts, not drained
1 (8 ounce) can tomato sauce
2 tablespoons red wine vinegar
2 tablespoons olive oil
1 teaspoon salt
¼ teaspoon pepper

Marinated Chicken and Pasta Salad

1 **pound corkscrew or fusilli pasta**
4 **chicken breasts, cooked and diced**
2 **(6 ounce) jars marinated artichoke hearts**
1 **avocado, sliced**
1-2 **tablespoons capers, drained**
1 **(3¼ ounce) jar sliced green olives**
2 **tomatoes, diced**
4 **scallions, chopped with some of green parts included**

Fresh Basil Dressing:
1 **cup fresh basil**
⅔ **cup olive oil**
  juice of one lemon
¼ **cup red wine vinegar**
1 **clove garlic, crushed**
1 **tablespoon Dijon mustard**
½ **teaspoon cayenne pepper**
  salt to taste

1. Cook pasta al dente, according to package directions; drain and cool. Add chicken, artichokes with marinade, avocado, capers, green olives, tomatoes and scallions.

2. Blend all ingredients for Fresh Basil Dressing in food processor or blender. Add to pasta-chicken mixture, toss well and chill for at least two hours before serving. Yield: 8 to 10 servings.

Curried Chicken Salad

1. Prepare all ingredients except the dressing and mix together in a large bowl.

2. Mix mayonnaise, yogurt and curry powder well. Pour over chicken and fruit mixture; mix well. Chill and serve on lettuce leaves. Yield: 10 to 12 servings.

4 chicken breasts, cooked and cubed
3 red apples, chopped
2 cups red seedless grapes
2 cups green seedless grapes
2 cups chopped celery
1 cup toasted whole almonds
1 cup raisins
½ cup raw sunflower seeds

Dressing:
1 cup mayonnaise
1 cup plain yogurt
3-5 teaspoons curry powder (according to taste)

Honey-Lemon Coleslaw

1. Blend together the mayonnaise, honey, lemon rind, lemon juice and ginger. Toss with cabbage and raisins. Cover and chill before serving. Yield: 6 to 8 servings.

½ cup mayonnaise
2 tablespoons honey
½ teaspoon grated lemon rind
2 tablespoons lemon juice
¼ teaspoon ground ginger
2 cups shredded red cabbage
2 cups shredded green cabbage
½ cup golden raisins (add ¼ cup more if you wish)

Classic Coleslaw

2　cups shredded cabbage
1　cup diced apples
½　cup chopped walnuts
½　cup grated carrots
¼　cup raisins
1　tablespoon sugar
½　teaspoon lemon juice
½　cup whipping cream
¼　cup mayonnaise

1. Combine cabbage, apples, nuts, raisins and carrots.

2. Mix together sugar, lemon juice, whipping cream and mayonnaise with wire whisk. Fold into cabbage mixture and combine well. Yield: 6 to 8 servings.

Mammoth Lakes Salad

2　heads butter lettuce, washed and dried
2　(11 ounce) cans mandarin oranges, drained
1　cup banana chips
¾　cup flaked coconut
¾　cup raisins
¾　cup peanuts
½　cup sunflower seeds

Poppyseed Dressing:
⅔　cup white wine vinegar
⅔　cup water
1　cup sugar (more to taste)
2　teaspoons dry mustard
½　teaspoon salt
⅔　cup vegetable oil
1　tablespoon poppyseeds

1. Tear lettuce into bite-sized pieces and put in salad bowl. Add drained oranges, banana chips, coconut, raisins, peanuts and sunflower seeds.

2. Make Poppyseed Dressing: Combine first 5 ingredients. Slowly add oil, whisking until thick. If too tart, add more sugar, 1 tablespoon at a time. Stir in poppyseeds. Yield: About 3 cups dressing.

3. Drizzle ½ cup dressing over salad, toss and serve. Yield: 8 servings.

Note: Poppyseed Dressing is good served on coleslaw with apples. Keeps in refrigerator for several weeks.

◊ Nutritional information per serving:

Calories 593	Fat .... 33 g	Iron .... 3 mg
Protein .... 8 g	Cholesterol .... 0 mg	Potassium .... 695 mg
Carbohydrates .... 75 g	Calcium .... 107 mg	Sodium .... 290 mg

Gazpacho Wreath

1. Combine gelatin and 1 cup of tomato juice in 2 quart pan, heat until gelatin dissolves.

2. Transfer gelatin mixture to a large bowl. Add remaining 2 cups of tomato juice, vinegar, garlic, salt, pepper and cayenne. Chill in refrigerator (or freezer for 20 to 30 minutes), until it begins to set.

3. While gelatin mixture is setting, peel tomatoes by covering with boiling water for 1 minute, cool for 1 minute, then peel. Seed and chop tomatoes, and combine with green onions, cucumber, celery and parsley. Refrigerate.

4. Spray a 9 or 10 inch ring mold with vegetable spray. When gelatin mixture is partially set, combine all ingredients and pour into mold. Chill until firm.

5. Combine all ingredients for Egg Salad and chill in refrigerator until ready to use.

6. When gelatin mold is firm, unmold on round plate and fill center with egg salad. Garnish outside with parsley. Serve with crackers. Yield: 6 to 8 servings.

2 envelopes unflavored gelatin
3 cups tomato juice
3 tablespoons wine vinegar
1 garlic clove, minced
1 teaspoon salt
¼ teaspoon pepper
   dash cayenne pepper
2 large tomatoes
¼ cup chopped green onion
¾ cup diced green pepper
¾ cup chopped cucumber
¾ cup diced celery
3 tablespoons chopped parsley

Egg Salad Stuffer:
6 hard cooked eggs
1 tablespoon prepared mustard
½ teaspoon salt
¼ cup mayonnaise
   dash pepper
½ teaspoon vinegar

Note: Makes a nice luncheon salad or may be served as an appetizer.

Coachella Salad

2 **sectioned grapefruit**
2 **sectioned oranges**
1 **(8 ounce) package cream cheese, cubed**
½ **cup Candied Ginger (see preparation method below)**
1 **cup pitted and chopped dates**
1 **large head green leaf lettuce**

Dressing:
¼ **medium yellow onion**
pinch of salt
4 **cups vegetable oil**
1 **cup honey**

1. Put all salad ingredients into a large mixing bowl.

2. Prepare the salad dressing: Puree the onion and salt in a food processor until very smooth. With motor running, add the oil very slowly. Add the honey and adjust sweetness to taste.

3. Pour desired amount of dressing over salad and toss lightly. The remaining dressing may be refrigerated and used another time on other fruit salads. Serve immediately on chilled plates. Yield: 4 servings.

Candied Ginger:
fresh ginger, cut into thin julienne strips
1 **cup brown sugar**
water

1. Boil ginger in lightly salted water for 10 minutes. Drain and rinse. Boil it again in clean water for 10 more minutes and rinse.

2. Boil sugar in a saucepan with just enough water to dissolve the sugar and to make a thick syrup. Add the ginger and boil one minute more. Set aside and cool.

Note: Recipe used with special permission from Cattails Restaurant, Cathedral City, California.

Orange and Onion Salad

1. Several hours before serving, peel and slice the oranges cross-wise very thinly. Place in a shallow bowl. Thinly slice red onion and separate into rings. Tuck in among orange slices.

2. Blend together vegetable oil, wine vinegar, sugar, paprika, salt and mustard. Pour dressing over orange and onion slices. Cover and refrigerate at least 2 hours.

3. To serve, lift orange and onion slices from dressing and arrange on lettuce-lined salad plates. Garnish with avocado slices. Serve remaining dressing in a small serving dish. Yield: 8 to 10 servings.

3-4 large oranges
1 large red onion
½ cup vegetable oil
¼ cup white wine vinegar
2 tablespoons sugar
¾ teaspoon paprika
½ teaspoon salt
¼ teaspoon dry mustard
romaine and red lettuce leaves
1 avocado, peeled and sliced

◊ Nutritional information per serving:

Calories	177	Fat	14 g	Iron	0.9 mg
Protein	2 g	Cholesterol	0 mg	Potassium	381 mg
Carbohydrates	13 g	Calcium	46 mg	Sodium	116 mg

Oriental Pasta Salad

1. Cook spaghetti to al dente and drain well.

2. Meanwhile, in saucepan, stir red pepper and oils over medium heat for 2 minutes. Add honey, soy sauce and salt. Stir to combine and mix well with cooked spaghetti. Cover and refrigerate for at least 4 hours, or overnight.

3. When ready to serve, add chopped cilantro, peanuts and green onions to noodles. Toss together and place in serving bowl. Sprinkle with sesame seeds and cilantro leaves for garnish. Yield: 8 to 10 servings.

1 pound spaghetti
2 teaspoons crushed dry red pepper
¼ cup corn oil
½ cup sesame oil
6 tablespoons honey
5 tablespoons soy sauce
1 teaspoon salt (optional)
½ cup chopped cilantro
¾ cup chopped peanuts
½ cup chopped green onions
2 tablespoons sesame seeds
cilantro leaves for garnish

Orange-Almond Salad

½ **head romaine lettuce, shredded**
1 **(11 ounce) can mandarin oranges**
1 **cup sliced celery**
2 **tablespoons minced parsley**
2 **green onions, sliced**
½ **cup sliced toasted almonds**

Dressing:
⅓ **cup vegetable oil**
3 **tablespoons tarragon vinegar**
2-3 **tablespoons sugar**
1-2 **drops of hot pepper sauce, according to taste**
½ **teaspoon salt**

1. Place lettuce, oranges, celery, parsley, onions and almonds in salad bowl.

2. Mix dressing and add to salad just before serving. Toss lightly. Yield: 6 to 8 servings.

◊ Nutritional information per serving:

Calories 175	Fat .... 15 g	Iron .... 0.93 mg
Protein .... 3 g	Cholesterol .... 0 mg	Potassium .... 222 mg
Carbohydrates .... 10 g	Calcium .... 43 mg	Sodium .... 152 mg

Romaine, Orange and Jicama Salad

1. In medium bowl, combine romaine, green onions, oranges, peppers and jicamas. Toss well and set aside.

2. In a small bowl, combine shallots, garlic, basil and vinegar. Whisk until blended. Slowly add oil in a stream and whisk until blended. Add salt and pepper and taste for seasonings. (Can be made in food processor.) Dressing will keep up to 1 week in refrigerator, remove from refrigerator one hour before using and whisk to blend well.

3. Before serving, pour dressing over salad and toss. Sprinkle with sunflower seeds. Yield: 6 to 8 servings.

2 **heads romaine lettuce, washed and broken into small pieces**
3 **green onions with tops, chopped**
2 **oranges, peeled and diced**
½ **red pepper, diced**
½ **yellow pepper, diced**
½ **jicama, julienned**
¼ **cup sunflower seeds**

Dressing:
2 **small shallots, finely chopped**
2 **garlic cloves, finely chopped**
½ **cup chopped fresh basil (optional)**
4 **tablespoons seasoned rice vinegar**
6 **tablespoons olive oil salt and pepper to taste**

Note: Great salad with a Mexican menu or barbecued foods.

◊ Nutritional information per serving:

Calories 169	Fat .... 13 g	Iron .... 1 mg
Protein .... 4 g	Cholesterol .... 0 mg	Potassium .... 502 mg
Carbohydrates .... 12 g	Calcium .... 91 mg	Sodium .... 47 mg

Fruit and Sesame Salad

1 **bunch watercress**
1 **papaya, sliced**
1 **avocado, peeled and sliced**
½ **jicama, julienne-sliced**
1 **mango, peeled and sliced**

Dressing:
⅓ **cup sesame seeds**
¼ **cup sugar**
¼ **teaspoon mustard (or 1 tablespoon Dijon mustard)**
¼ **teaspoon hot pepper sauce**
½ **teaspoon paprika**
½ **teaspoon salt**
½ **teaspoon Worcestershire sauce**
3 **tablespoons minced onion**
½ **cup wine vinegar**

1. Mix dressing ingredients together. Chill for at least 2 hours before serving.

2. Arrange fruit slices and watercress on large platter or individual salad plates. Pour dressing over fruit. Serve immediately. Yield: 6 servings.

◊ Nutritional information per serving:

Calories 189	Fat .... 9 g	Iron .... 2 mg
Protein .... 3 g	Cholesterol .... 0 mg	Potassium .... 492 mg
Carbohydrates .... 27 g	Calcium .... 118 mg	Sodium .... 231 mg

Pasta Salad with Shrimp and Broccoli

1. Cook pasta al dente (for added flavor add 2 tablespoons chicken bouillon granules to cooking water), drain. Cook broccoli to tender-crisp stage, adding 2 tablespoons chicken bouillon granules to water (optional). Combine pasta, broccoli, tomatoes, onion, shrimp, and cheese in a bowl.

2. Blend dressing ingredients well with a wire whisk, and pour over salad. Mix well and chill before serving. Yield: 10 servings.

½ pound mostaciolli pasta
2 cups broccoli flowerets
2 tomatoes, diced
1 red onion, diced
½ pound shrimp
1 cup grated Parmesan cheese

Dressing:
¾ cup olive oil
4 tablespoons chopped fresh basil
2 cloves garlic, mashed
1½ tablespoons lemon juice
¼ teaspoon grated lemon peel
3 tablespoons chopped fresh parsley

Pasta Salad with Lime Vinaigrette

1. Mix ingredients for Lime Vinaigrette dressing in a small bowl. Cover and let stand for 2 hours.

2. Cook pasta in boiling water according to package directions. Drain and cool.

3. Add chopped tomatoes, black olives and cilantro. Toss.

4. Remove garlic from dressing, whisk lightly and add to pasta ingredients. Toss to coat well. Yield: 6 to 8 servings.

8 ounces small shell pasta (preferably 4 ounces spinach and 4 ounces plain)
3 medium tomatoes, finely chopped
1 (2.2 ounce) can sliced black olives
4-5 tablespoons chopped cilantro

Lime Vinaigrette Dressing:
6 tablespoons olive oil
2 garlic cloves, lightly crushed
2 tablespoons lime juice salt and freshly ground pepper to taste

Note: If using as a main dish, add crab or shrimp (cooked) and extra lemon or lime juice.

Hearty Tossed Salad

2 tablespoons melted butter
1 teaspoon garlic salt
1 teaspoon curry powder
2 teaspoons Worcestershire sauce
1 (4½ ounce) can Chinese noodles
1 head romaine lettuce, broken into bite-sized pieces
½ head iceberg lettuce, shredded (spinach, butter, or other greens may be used instead)
1 cup bean sprouts
2 tomatoes, diced
8 slices bacon, cooked, drained and crumbled
2 hard boiled eggs
mushrooms, sliced (optional)
1 green pepper, sliced (optional)

Dressing:
1 cup vegetable oil
¼ cup sugar (or ½ cup, according to taste)
⅔ cup catsup
¼ cup vinegar
2 tablespoons minced onion
2 teaspoons Worcestershire sauce

1. Melt butter, add garlic salt, curry powder, Worcestershire sauce and mix well. Add Chinese noodles and toss until noodles are well coated. Spread noodles in a single layer on a cookie sheet and bake at 250° for 15 minutes. Remove from oven and cool. This can be done ahead of time and stored in an airtight container until ready to use.

2. Combine all salad dressing ingredients in blender or food processor and blend well.

3. Just before serving, combine the lettuces, sprouts, tomatoes, bacon, eggs, mushrooms and green peppers. Pour just enough salad dressing over to coat lightly. Toss well. Add Chinese noodles to salad and toss again. The rest of the dressing may be stored in the refrigerator for another use. Yield: 8 servings.

Note: This is a very hearty salad that goes well with barbecued chicken or ribs. Add cooked chicken or diced ham to the salad and it becomes a meal in itself.

Marinated Rice Salad

1. Cook the rice according to directions, cool. Blend together vinaigrette marinade and mix with cooked and cooled rice. Cover and refrigerate overnight.

2. Add the vegetables and optional tuna to the rice mixture and chill until ready to serve. Yield: 6 servings

1 **cup long-grain rice**
1 **cucumber, peeled, seeded and diced**
1 **green pepper, finely diced**
2 **green onions, finely chopped**
3 **ounces stuffed green olives, very thinly sliced**
1 **large tomato, diced**
1 **(6 ounce) can water-packed tuna, flaked (optional)**

Vinaigrette Marinade:
½ **cup red wine vinegar**
¼ **cup olive oil**
¼ **cup vegetable oil**
1 **tablespoon Dijon mustard**
⅛ **teaspoon garlic powder dash salt**

◊ Nutritional information per serving:

Calories 343	Fat ....21 g	Iron ....2 mg
Protein ....11 g	Cholesterol ....16 mg	Potassium ....295 mg
Carbohydrates ....30 g	Calcium ....33 mg	Sodium ....476 mg

Shrimp Walnut Salad

1 **tablespoon butter**
1 **tablespoon soy sauce**
1 **cup walnut halves**
1 **cup diagonally sliced celery**
½ **cup sliced green onions**
1 **(5 ounce) can water chestnuts, drained and sliced**
1 **(11 ounce) can mandarin oranges, drained**
2 **pounds cooked shrimp crisp salad greens**

Sweet and Sour Dressing:
1 **cup vegetable oil**
½ **cup sugar**
¼ **cup vinegar**
1 **tablespoon Worcestershire sauce**
⅓ **cup catsup**

1. Melt butter, add soy sauce and walnuts. Stir gently over low heat until walnuts are lightly toasted, about 10 minutes. Remove from heat, spread on paper towels and allow to cool. Mix celery, onions, water chestnuts, orange segments and shrimp.

2. Blend together dressing ingredients and toss with shrimp and walnut mixture. Place on salad greens and serve with additional dressing, if desired. Yield: 4 to 6 servings.

Summer Rice Salad

2 **cups cooked white long grain rice, cooled**
1 **cup frozen peas, cooked and cooled**
½ **cup sliced celery**
¼ **cup chopped green onions**
½ **cup fresh chopped tomatoes, drained**
⅔ **cup mayonnaise**
⅔ **cup sour cream**
   salt and pepper to taste

1. Combine rice, peas, celery, green onions, tomatoes, salt and pepper. Mix mayonnaise and sour cream and gently fold into rice mixture. Yield: 6 servings.

Optional: Add 2 cups diced cooked chicken, ham, crabmeat or shrimp (add 2 tablespoons lemon juice if you use shrimp or crabmeat).

Spinach-Apple-Bacon Toss

1. Toast almonds at 350° for 5 minutes, cool. Combine with spinach, bacon, and onions in a medium bowl.

2. Blend together salad dressing ingredients. Dice apple and add to salad bowl, pour just enough dressing over salad to cover leaves. Toss well. Serve the remaining dressing on the side. Yield: 6 to 8 servings.

⅓ cup sliced almonds
1 large bunch spinach, washed and torn into bite-sized pieces
6 strips bacon, cooked crisp and crumbled
3 tablespoons sliced green onion
1 large red apple

Dressing:
½ cup vegetable oil
6 tablespoons tarragon wine vinegar
¼ teaspoon salt
2 teaspoons sugar
1 teaspoon dry mustard
¼ teaspoon ground pepper

◊ Nutritional information per serving:

Calories 200	Fat ....18 g	Iron ....,... 1 mg
Protein ....8 g	Cholesterol ....4 mg	Potassium ....259 mg
Carbohydrates ....8 g	Calcium ....44 mg	Sodium ....174 mg

Feta-Spinach Salad

2 bunches fresh spinach,
washed, dried and torn
into bite-sized pieces
8 slices bacon, cooked
crisp and crumbled
½ pound fresh mush-
rooms, sliced
¼ pound feta cheese,
crumbled
croutons (optional)

Dressing:
1 tablespoon vinegar
1 tablespoon lemon juice
6 tablespoons olive oil
1 teaspoon Dijon mustard
2 tablespoons grated
onion, or 3-4 green
onions, sliced
½ teaspoon freshly ground
pepper

1. Combine spinach, bacon, mushrooms and feta cheese in a large
bowl.

2. Whisk together dressing ingredients and pour over spinach. Toss well
and serve. Yield: 6 servings.

Strawberry-Spinach Salad

1 pint strawberries, thickly
sliced
1 bunch fresh spinach,
torn into bite-sized
pieces
½ red onion, thickly sliced

Dressing:
½ cup mayonnaise
2 tablespoons white
vinegar or 1 tablespoon
lemon juice plus 1
tablespoon vinegar
⅓ cup sugar
¼ cup whole milk
2 tablespoons poppy
seeds

1. Toss strawberries, spinach and red
onion in bowl.

2. Blend together dressing ingredients and add to strawberry-spinach
mixture. Serve immediately. Yield: 4
to 6 servings.

Tomato-Cucumber Country Salad

1. Combine lettuce, tomatoes, cucumbers, onion, green pepper and olives in a medium bowl.

2. Whisk together the oil, vinegar, salt, pepper and oregano to blend thoroughly. Just before serving, pour over salad ingredients and toss. Sprinkle with feta cheese. Yield: 6 to 8 servings.

1 **small head lettuce, torn into bite-sized pieces**
10 **small tomatoes, cut into bite-sized pieces**
3 **cucumbers, peeled and sliced**
2 **small red onions, thinly sliced**
1 **green pepper, sliced**
24 **olives, black or green**
½ **pound feta cheese, crumbled**

Dressing:
½ **cup olive oil**
3 **tablespoons red wine vinegar**
½ **teaspoon salt**
⅛ **teaspoon freshly ground pepper**
½ **teaspoon dried oregano**

◊ Nutritional information per serving:

Calories 276	Fat .... 24 g	Iron .... 2 mg
Protein .... 7 g	Cholesterol .... 25 mg	Potassium .... 607 mg
Carbohydrates .... 14 g	Calcium .... 198 mg	Sodium .... 574 mg

Kenwood Restaurant's Sweetbread Salad

1 **pound veal or calf sweetbreads**
2 **tablespoons lemon juice**
32 **leaves of young green lettuce (arugula, oakleaf, romaine)**
16 **leaves of Belgian endive**
16 **medium-sized button mushrooms, sliced thin**
1 **cup French vinaigrette (purchased)**
1 **tablespoon olive oil**
1 **cup veal stock (canned beef stock can be substituted)**
4 **tablespoons capers**
1 **tablespoon chopped parsley**
2 **tablespoons very finely chopped celery**

1. Cook sweetbreads in water with 2 tablespoons lemon juice for 5 minutes over medium heat. Allow them to cool in water. When cool, remove from water and remove all nerves, etc., then cut into 1 inch pieces.

2. Garnish 4 plates with lettuce, endive and mushrooms around the perimeter. Season the lettuce with the vinaigrette.

3. In saute pan, heat the oil to medium heat, then saute the sweetbreads until light brown and crispy. Remove with slotted spoon and discard oil. Arrange in the middle of the lettuce garnished plate.

4. Deglaze pan with beefstock, add capers and bring to a boil. Pour sauce on top of sweetbreads. Sprinkle with parsley and celery. Serve immediately. Yield: 4 servings.

Note: Recipe used with special permission from Kenwood's Restaurant, Kenwood City, California.

California Taco Salad

1. Cook, drain, crumble and cool ground beef.

2. Combine the dressing ingredients and toss with the salad ingredients in a large bowl. Garnish with chopped cilantro if desired. Yield: 10 to 12 servings.

Dressing:
- 2 cups sour cream
- 20-25 drops hot pepper sauce
- 1 teaspoon garlic salt
- 1 teaspoon pepper
- 1 clove garlic, minced
- 2 tablespoons mayonnaise
- ½ cup catsup
- ½ cup hot taco sauce

Salad:
- 1 pound ground beef
- 1 medium head iceberg lettuce, chopped
- 1 can chili beans (not con carne), drained
- 1 pound sharp Cheddar, shredded
- 1 red onion, chopped
- 2 avocados, cut into ½ inch pieces
- 2 tomatoes, cut into ½ inch pieces
- 1 (2.2 ounce) can sliced black olives, drained
- ½ package plain tortilla chips, slightly crushed (or more to taste) chopped cilantro (optional)

Lemon Mustard Dressing

1 cup vegetable oil
2½ tablespoons lemon juice
4 teaspoons Dijon mustard
¾ teaspoon pepper
2 tablespoons fresh, chopped chives or ½ teaspoon dried chives

1. Put all ingredients in blender or food processor and process until well mixed. Yield: 1½ cups.

Note: Good on tossed green salad, also as a basting sauce for chicken or fish.

Italian Herb Vinaigrette

¾ cup olive oil
½ cup balsamic vinegar
1½ teaspoons garlic salt
1 teaspoon MSG
2 tablespoons fresh basil leaves or ½ teaspoon dried
½ teaspoon oregano leaves
1½ teaspoons salt
½ teaspoon pepper

1. Combine all ingredients in a jar with a lid. Shake well to blend. Refrigerate, covered, and shake well before using. Yield: 1 cup.

Sesame Vinaigrette

1 cup light olive oil
½ cup cider vinegar
¼ cup sugar, ¼ cup more if preferred
½ tablespoon Worcestershire sauce
1 teaspoon onion juice
¼ teaspoon dry mustard
½ teaspoon salt
½ teaspoon paprika
¼ cup toasted sesame seeds

1. Place all ingredients except sesame seeds in blender and blend well. Before serving, add seeds to salad and toss. Yield: 2 cups.

Creamy Vinaigrette

1. Mix the ingredients in the order given in a jar with a tight-fitting lid. Shake thoroughly to blend. Let sit for at least one hour to allow flavors to blend. Shake well before using. Yield: 1¼ cups.

- 1 clove garlic, crushed
- 1 teaspoon salt
- 1 tablespoon Dijon mustard
- 1 tablespoon coarse black pepper (or less, according to taste)
- 2 tablespoons minced fresh parsley
- 1 hard-boiled egg, sieved
- ⅔ cup olive oil
- ⅓ cup red wine vinegar
- 2 tablespoons heavy cream

Ranch Dressing

1. Place all ingredients except sour cream in a jar with a tight-fitting lid and shake well.

2. Add sour cream and shake. Yield: 2¼ cups.

- 1½ cups vegetable oil
- 2 tablespoons tarragon vinegar
- 2 tablespoons lemon juice
- 3 teaspoons chopped onion
- 3 teaspoons chopped parsley
- 3 teaspoons sugar
- 1 teaspoon mustard seed
- 1 teaspoon celery seed
- ½ teaspoon thyme
- 1 clove garlic, minced
- ½ cup sour cream

Basil Mayonnaise

½ **cup vegetable oil**
1 **tablespoon vinegar**
  (white or white wine)
1 **egg**
¾ **teaspoon salt**
½ **teaspoon dry mustard**
  (or 1 tablespoon Dijon
  mustard)
¼ **teaspoon paprika**
⅛ **teaspoon pepper**
1 **bunch (or 1 cup)**
  chopped basil leaves
  (must use fresh basil)
½ **cup olive oil**
1 **tablespoon vinegar**

1. In food processor or blender, process: vegetable oil, vinegar, egg, seasonings and basil leaves.

2. Slowly add olive oil, drop by drop, then 1 tablespoon vinegar.

3. If mayonnaise fails (rarely!), start over with another egg and 1 table-spoon vinegar, then add the whole (failed) first mixture.

Note: Mayonnaise recipe is superior to store bought. Great on grilled chicken breasts, tomato slices, grilled sausage sandwiches, fresh green beans.

Breads

BREAD AND PIZZA

Bread and pizza deserve a rich, young red wine to make it shine. The ingredients of the pizza sauce and the flavor of the additions will obliterate anything subtle. A good Zinfandel, which is something like the California answer to Chianti, is the Number One choice.

Never-To-Be-Forgotten Garlic Loaf

1. Cut bread in half lengthwise; tear out soft center of bread in chunks, leaving crust intact. Put shell on baking sheet covered with foil.

2. Melt butter in large skillet, stir in garlic and sesame seeds. Add bread chunks and cook until golden and butter is absorbed. Remove from heat.

3. Combine sour cream, Jack cheese, Parmesan cheese, parsley and lemon pepper. Stir in artichoke hearts and toasted bread. Mix well and spoon into bread shells. Sprinkle with Cheddar cheese. Bake at 350° for 30 minutes.

4. This could make a light meal, served with a green salad. Left-over, it can be reheated in a microwave for a very short time. Yield: 1 loaf.

1 (1 pound) loaf French bread
6 tablespoons butter or margarine
2-8 cloves fresh garlic, crushed (amount of garlic depending on taste)
7 teaspoons sesame seeds
1½ cups sour cream
2 cups Monterey Jack or mozzarella cheese (small cubes)
¼ cup grated Parmesan cheese
2 tablespoons parsley, minced
2 teaspoons lemon pepper
1 (14 ounce) can artichoke hearts, drained and coarsely chopped (not marinated)
1 cup shredded Cheddar cheese

Orange-Macadamia Nut Bread

1 cup butter or ½ cup butter and ½ cup margarine
1 cup sugar
1 tablespoon orange rind, grated
2 tablespoons orange juice
4 eggs (room temperature)
2 cups flour
¼ teaspoon baking powder
½ cup Macadamia nuts, chopped

1. Cream butter and margarine. Slowly add sugar. Beat in orange rind and orange juice.

2. Beat in one egg at a time, mixing well in between. Sift flour and baking powder together and add all at once to creamed mixture. Add chopped Macadamia nuts.

3. Pour into 4 or 5 greased and floured 3x6 inch bread pans, or 18 muffin tins. Decorate tops with 2 or 3 whole Macadamia nuts.

4. For bread: Bake 20 minutes at 350°. Reduce heat to 300° and bake 10 minutes longer. For muffins, bake 25 minutes at 350°. Yield: 4 or 5 (3x6 inch) loaves, or 18 muffins.

California Avocado Bread

½ cup butter
1 cup sugar
1 cup mashed avocado
2 eggs, well beaten
2 teaspoons lemon juice
2 teaspoons baking powder
1½ cups flour
½ teaspoon salt
½ teaspoon cloves, ground
dash cinnamon
1 cup walnuts, chopped

1. Mix avocado with beaten eggs.

2. Cream butter and sugar together and mix all ingredients in order given.

3. Pour batter into a 9x5 inch greased and floured loaf pan. Bake at 350° for 15 minutes.

4. Lower oven to 325° and bake for another 45 minutes.

5. Cool on rack. Yield: 1 (9x5 inch) loaf.

Banana-Blueberry Bread

1. Cream shortening. Add sugar gradually, beating until light and fluffy. Add the eggs, one at a time, beating well after each addition. Mix in the mashed banana.

2. In another bowl, combine the remaining ingredients, stirring gently. Add the two mixtures, stirring just until moist. Spoon batter in a greased and sugared loaf pan.

3. Bake at 350° for 50 to 55 minutes or until wooden toothpick inserted comes out clean.

4. Cool in the pan for about 10 minutes; remove from pan and cool completely on wire rack. Yield: 1 (9x5 inch) loaf.

½ cup shortening
1 cup sugar
2 eggs
1 cup mashed banana
½ cup uncooked, quick-cooking oats
½ cup chopped pecans
1½ cups flour
¼ teaspoon salt
1 teaspoon baking soda
1 cup fresh or frozen, well-drained blueberries

Bubble Bread

1. Combine pudding mix, brown sugar, cinnamon and chopped nuts. Blend well and put half of the mixture into greased 12 cup Bundt pan.

2. Layer rolls on top of dry ingredients, sprinkling dry ingredients between the layers. Drizzle the butter over rolls. Cover with a towel and let rise. (Can be assembled at night and baked in the morning.)

3. Bake for 30 to 40 minutes at 350°. While still warm, invert pan onto serving dish. Let stand until bread releases. Remove pan. Yield: 8 servings.

1 (3⅝ ounce) package butterscotch pudding
½ cup brown sugar
1 teaspoon cinnamon
1 cup chopped walnuts
1 (25 ounce) bag frozen Parker House style rolls (use about ⅔)
½ cup butter or margarine, melted

Bran Muffins

2 cups shreds of wheat bran cereal
2 cups boiling water
1 cup margarine, softened
2½ cups sugar
8 egg whites, beaten
1 quart buttermilk
5 cups flour
3 tablespoons baking soda
1 tablespoon salt
4 cups bran flake cereal
2 cups raisins

1. Soften shreds of wheat bran cereal in boiling water, set aside.

2. Cream butter, sugar and eggs. Add the scalded bran, then the buttermilk, blending well after each addition. Add the flour, baking soda and salt to the liquid mixture, mixing well. Stir in the bran flakes, then the raisins.

3. Cover tightly and refrigerate overnight or for about 12 hours before making the first batch of muffins.

4. Do not stir the mixture before spooning into muffin tins. Carefully fill muffin tins about ⅔ full.

5. Bake at 400° for about 20 minutes. (If using the mini muffin tins bake for 10 minutes.)

6. This mixture may be kept in the refrigerator for up to six weeks and baked when convenient. Remember not to stir the mixture. Or, muffins may be baked all at once and frozen. Reheat only what is needed in the microwave (about 40 seconds per muffin, do not overheat or they will be tough). Yield: About 60 muffins.

Optional: Add 1 cup of chopped nuts or cut up dates to recipe. Four whole eggs may be used instead of 8 egg whites. Recipe will taste the same but will be higher in cholesterol.

◊ Nutritional information per serving:

Calories 135	Fat .... 3.6 g	Iron .... 1.25 mg
Protein .... 3 g	Cholesterol .... 0.6 mg	Potassium .... 147 mg
Carbohydrates ...... 24.9 g	Calcium .... 30 mg	Sodium .... 321 mg

Apricot Lemon Muffins

1. Combine milk and apricots and set aside to soften.

2. Stir together flours, sugar, baking powder, salt and lemon zest.

3. Blend oil, egg, milk and apricots.

4. Mix dry and liquid ingredients together and allow to sit about 10 minutes.

5. Fill greased muffin tins ⅔ full.

6. Bake 20 to 25 minutes at 400°. Remove from oven and let muffins sit in pan for 5 minutes. Remove and cool on a wire rack. Yield: 12 to 18 muffins.

1½ **cups milk**
½ **cup chopped dried apricots**
1¼ **cups flour**
1 **cup whole wheat flour**
½ **cup sugar**
1 **tablespoon baking powder**
1 **teaspoon salt**
2 **teaspoons grated lemon zest**
1 **egg, beaten**
½ **cup vegetable oil**

◊ Nutritional information per serving:

Calories	133	Fat	7.1 g	Iron	0.6 mg
Protein	2 g	Cholesterol	14.2 mg	Potassium	93.6 mg
Carbohydrates	16 g	Calcium	39 mg	Sodium	187 mg

Apple Muffins

1. Combine flour, apples, sugar, salt, soda and cinnamon in large bowl.

2. Stir in oil, nuts and vanilla. (Batter will be stiff.)

3. Fill greased and floured muffin tins about ½ to ⅔ full. Bake at 350° for 30 minutes, or until a toothpick inserted in the center comes out clean. Yield: 24 muffins.

3½ **cups all purpose flour**
3 **cups finely chopped, peeled apples (preferably green, tart apples)**
2 **cups sugar**
1 **teaspoon salt**
1 **teaspoon baking soda**
1 **teaspoon cinnamon**
1½ **cups vegetable oil**
½ **cup toasted, chopped nuts**
1 **teaspoon vanilla**

Dilly Cheese Bread

1 **package dry yeast**
½ **cup warm water**
1 **cup creamed cottage cheese**
2 **tablespoons sugar**
1 **tablespoon finely chopped onion**
1 **tablespoon butter**
2 **tablespoons dill weed**
1 **teaspoon salt**
¼ **teaspoon soda**
1 **egg**
2¼ **cups flour**

1. Dissolve yeast in warm water. Stir in cottage cheese that has been heated to lukewarm.

2. In a large bowl, combine all ingredients and yeast, except flour. Add flour gradually until a stiff dough is formed, beating well after each addition.

3. Cover bowl with a lightly dampened towel and let dough rise in a warm place (85° to 98°) for 50 to 60 minutes, or until doubled in bulk.

4. Punch down, turn into a well-buttered 1½ or 2 quart round casserole or loaf pan and let rise for 30 to 40 minutes.

5. Bake 40 to 50 minutes at 350°. Remove from oven and let rest for 15 minutes then brush with butter and sprinkle with coarse salt. Let cool in pan. Yield: 1 loaf.

◊ Nutritional information per serving:

Calories 76	Fat ....1.4 g	Iron ....0.89 mg
Protein ....3.3 g	Cholesterol ....13.5 mg	Potassium ....44 mg
Carbohydrates ....4.2 g	Calcium.................16 mg	Sodium ....169 mg

Italian Rolls

1. Put flour, salt and butter in a food processor with a dough blade. Run for 45 seconds. Add yeast and water mixture and sugar in a steady stream. Process until ball is formed, about 60 seconds.

2. Let rise, covered in oiled bowl, until doubled. Form into egg-sized balls and place on greased baking sheet that has been sprinkled with cornmeal. Brush with olive oil and let rise, covered with plastic wrap.

3. Bake at 425° for 12 to 13 minutes with a pan of water on a lower shelf in the oven.

4. Brush with egg whites and bake 5 minutes longer, or until golden brown. Yield: 12 to 18 rolls.

2 packages yeast, dissolved in 1¾ cups warm water
1½ teaspoons salt
1 tablespoon margarine or butter
1 tablespoon sugar
5 cups flour
1 egg white, beaten with 1 tablespoon water
¼ cup cornmeal
2 tablespoons olive oil

◊ Nutritional information per serving:

Calories 154	Fat .... 2.6 g	Iron .... 1.7 mg
Protein .... 4.3 g	Cholesterol .... 1.72 mg	Potassium .... 56 mg
Carbohydrates .... 28 g	Calcium .... 7.9 mg	Sodium .... 188 mg

Quick-Rising Sweet Dough

¾ **cup milk, scalded**
½ **cup butter, melted**
¾ **cup water**
3 **packages yeast**
¼ **teaspoon pectin**
½ **cup sugar**
1½ **teaspoons salt**
2 **eggs**
5½ **cups flour**

Quantities for 48 Rolls:
1½ **cups milk**
½ **pound butter**
1½ **cups water**
4 **packages yeast**
¼ **teaspoon pectin**
1 **cup sugar**
1 **tablespoon salt**
4 **eggs**
11 **cups flour**

Quantities for 70 Rolls:
2½ **cups milk**
¾ **pound butter**
2½ **cups water**
5 **packages yeast**
¼ **teaspoon pectin**
1½ **cups sugar**
4½ **teaspoons salt**
6 **eggs**
16 **cups flour**

Cinnamon Rolls:
   melted butter
   brown sugar
   granulated sugar
   cinnamon
   chopped nuts

1. Mix together milk and butter and let cool for 15 minutes. Dissolve yeast in lukewarm water and add to milk-butter mixture. Add pectin (aids in the growth of the yeast). Set aside to ripen for about 5 minutes.

2. In large bowl, mix sugar, salt and eggs; stir well. Add milk mixture and yeast mixture. Stir again. Add flour a little bit at a time, while stirring constantly. Start kneading when dough becomes a soft round ball. Knead until smooth and elastic, about 8 minutes. Slowly add handfuls of flour as you are kneading so that dough will not stick to your fingers.

3. Place dough in a bowl that has been greased; turn the dough to grease it on all sides. Cover with towel; let rise in a warm, draft-free place until doubled in bulk (about 30 minutes). When doubled, punch down and place on a lightly floured surface.

4. Shape into dinner rolls, braided rolls or any interesting shapes desired. Let rise for another 30 minutes. Bake 12 to 15 minutes at 400°. Yield: 24 rolls.

1. For cinnamon rolls, take ½ of the dough (for 24 quantity) and roll into a rectangle. Spread with melted butter, sprinkle with brown sugar, granulated sugar, cinnamon, and chopped nuts. Roll up and cut into ¾ to 1 inch slices and bake. Repeat with other half of dough.

San Francisco Spread

1. Mix butter, mayonnaise and garlic salt.

2. Spread bread halves with above mixture; sprinkle with Parmesan cheese and paprika.

3. Place on baking sheet and bake for 10 minutes at 350°.

½ cup butter
½ cup mayonnaise
⅛ teaspoon garlic salt
½ cup Parmesan cheese
1 teaspoon paprika
1 loaf sourdough French
   or Italian bread, split
   lengthwise

Optional: Add 1 bunch green onions, chopped, to butter-mayonnaise mixture, plus 1 tablespoon Worcestershire sauce or add ½ cup shredded Cheddar cheese to butter-mayonnaise, then garnish with minced fresh parsley.

Orange-Nut Bread

1. Squeeze juice from orange; add enough boiling water to make 1 cup. Combine raisins or dates with orange zest to make one cup; mix with orange juice.

2. Stir in the following: soda, sugar, melted shortening, vanilla. In a separate bowl blend together egg, flour, baking powder and salt. Combine the ingredients of both bowls. Stir in the chopped nuts.

3. Place in one, greased 9x5 inch loaf pan. Bake 30 to 35 minutes at 350°. Check by inserting toothpick in center of pan. Remove from oven when toothpick comes out clean.

4. Serve with cream cheese, butter, or orange-flavored butter. Yield: 1 (9x5 inch) loaf.

1 fresh orange
¾ cup raisins or dates
   zest of 1 orange
1 teaspoon soda
¾ cup sugar
2 teaspoons melted
   shortening
1 teaspoon vanilla
1 egg, beaten
2 cups flour
1 teaspoon baking pow-
   der
½ teaspoon salt
½ cup chopped nuts

Alligator Bread

1½ cups warm water
1 package dry yeast
¼ cup sugar
1 teaspoon salt
¼ cup white vinegar
6 cups flour (approxi-
mately)

1. Pour water into bowl and sprinkle the yeast over the top. Sprinkle the sugar over it, causing the yeast to sink. Stir in 2 cups of the flour and wait until it develops bubbles (about 30 minutes).

2. Stir in the vinegar and salt, then about 4 more cups of the flour, until the dough is fairly stiff. Sprinkle flour generously on the counter and turn the dough out. Knead it well, adding flour as needed. Place dough in an oiled bowl (3 to 4 quart size) and oil the top. Cover with plastic wrap and put in a warm place for about 2 hours, until it doubles in bulk.

3. Turn dough out on a board and press into a square shape. Cut into 4 pieces.

4. To shape the alligators:

LEGS: Cut off a piece of dough about an inch wide and 4 inches long from the piece you are working with. Cut this in half and pull and twist each piece out until it is about 5 inches long. Lay the two pieces down on a greased cookie sheet.

BODY: Pull the remaining piece so that it is about 9 inches square. Roll up, starting at a corner. Lay on top of the legs. One end will be fatter than the other, so make this end the head. Pull the tail a bit to make it longer and thinner and give it a nice alligator-ish curve. Bend the legs.

DETAILS: With a sharp knife, cut criss-crosses on the body for that genuine alligator-hide effect. With scissors, facing alligator head on, cut where the mouth should be and place a large piece of foil, folded several times, in the mouth. Foil should be stiff enough so that it holds the jaws open. Place nuts or raisins for the eyes.

5. Brush with glaze and sprinkle with poppy seeds, if desired. Bake at 375° for 10 minutes. Quickly glaze again and bake for 20 minutes longer. Yield: 4 'Gators.

Glaze:
1 **beaten egg**
2 **tablespoons water**
1 **tablespoon Worcester-shire sauce**
  pine nuts, raisins, almonds or sunflower seeds for decoration

Cranberry Bread

1. Sift together flour, sugar, salt, baking powder and baking soda.

2. Add walnuts; orange rind, cranberries and orange juice.

3. Beat together eggs, buttermilk and oil. Add to dough and pour into a greased and floured (9x5 inch) loaf pan.

4. Bake 1½ hours at 325°. Let cool in pan. Can also be baked in 3 small loaf pans. Yield: 1 (9x5 inch) loaf.

3¼ **cups flour**
2 **cups sugar**
½ **teaspoon salt**
1½ **teaspoons baking powder**
1½ **teaspoons baking soda**
1 **cup chopped walnuts**
  grated rinds from 2 oranges
3 **cups fresh cranberries**
½ **cup orange juice**
2 **large eggs**
1 **cup buttermilk**
1 **cup vegetable oil**

Pizza

2 packages dry yeast
2½ cups very warm water
½ teaspoon sugar
1 teaspoon salt
1 tablespoon olive oil
5-6 cups unbleached flour

1. Dissolve the yeast in very warm water with sugar until it bubbles.

2. In a food processor fitted with the dough blade, or an electric mixer fitted with a dough hook, combine the yeast mixture with 1 cup of the flour, the salt and the olive oil. Mix well. Add the remaining flour ½ cup at a time until the dough forms a light, non-sticky ball.

3. Place dough in a large, well oiled ceramic bowl. Put enough additional olive oil on top of dough and turn dough to coat it completely. Cover with plastic wrap, sealing it well and placing it in a warm place to rise until doubled.

4. Preheat oven to 450°. Punch dough down, cutting into two equal pieces. Flatten each piece out on a well oiled 10x15 inch baking sheet. Push the dough out and into the corners of the baking sheet to make a slight border to hold the topping. (If it is difficult to flatten the dough, let it rest a few minutes and it will relax.)

5. Cover with plastic wrap again and let rise for 30 minutes.

6. Sprinkle with desired toppings (see suggestions). Bake pizza for about 20 minutes at 425° to 450°, until golden brown on bottom. Yield: 2 (10x15 inch) or 2 (12 inch round) pizzas.

Suggested Toppings:

1. Slice and saute 2 large red onions in 2 tablespoons olive oil plus 2 tablespoons butter, 2 cloves minced garlic, ½ to 1 teaspoon dried red pepper flakes and two sprigs fresh rosemary. Sprinkle on pizza dough and bake as usual.

2. Drizzle pizza with oil that has been flavored with garlic and rosemary. Sprinkle salt over the oiled dough and bake as usual.

3. Saute onions, green pepper and garlic. Top with grated Monterey Jack cheese and bake.

4. Mix a can of tomato puree, add one crushed garlic clove and fresh basil to flavor. Spread mixture on pizza and top with Monterey Jack cheese.

Pizza Rustica

1 **recipe pizza dough (see previous recipe) with 1 tablespoon extra olive oil added**

Filling:
2 **pounds ricotta cheese**
4 **egg yolks**
¼ **pound Monterey Jack cheese, grated**
½ **cup Parmesan, grated**
¼ **pound ham, cubed or ¼ pound prosciutto, cubed fresh parsley, chopped**
¼ **teaspoon grated fresh nutmeg**
   salt to taste
   fresh ground pepper to taste

1. Make dough according to directions. Let rise and punch down. Divide into two pieces.

2. Combine the ingredients for the filling. (Can be made ahead and refrigerated.)

3. Roll out dough on 2 large (10x15 inch) well oiled cookie sheets. Spread filling on one, leaving 1 inch around the edge free. Take the second cookie sheet of dough and flip over on top of the filled dough. The dough will gently cover the other (remove the top cookie sheet). Crimp the edges tightly to enclose the filling. Poke holes in the top, dot with butter.

4. Bake at 375° for 30 to 35 minutes. Cool on a rack, slice and serve.

Note: This is a wonderful holiday breakfast meal, served with fresh fruit, sliced prosciutto or salami, and hard-boiled eggs.

Pizza Rustica can be made ahead, cooled and refrigerated until ready to serve. Reheat in 325° oven for 10 minutes. Slice and serve.

California is a true microcosm in every sense of the word. Come visit with us the 12 spectacular regions which make California so wonderfully unique.

- The vast recreational opportunities of the Shasta-Cascade

- The rugged cliffs and the crashing surf of the Central Coast

- The highly contrasting geography of the Deserts

- The meandering Delta and agricultural cornucopia of the Central Valley

- The warm climate and sandy beaches of San Diego County

- The Inland Empire's high mountain lakes

- Greater Los Angeles, the home of Hollywood's brightest stars

- The world-famous theme parks of Orange County

- The colorful '49ers history of Gold Country

- The lush vineyards and giant redwoods of the North Coast

- The cosmopolitan diversity of the San Francisco Bay Area

- The unparalleled grandeur of the High Sierra

The majestic coast redwoods thrive along the foggy California coast from Redwood National Park south to Monterey County. These giants of nature often reach heights of over 300 feet. ▶

Sue Tushingham McNary ©59

SHASTA-CASCADE

Visitors to the vast, magnificent wilderness of the Shasta-Cascade never would guess that California is the most populous state in the nation. This is big country, with snow-capped mountains, volcanoes, glaciers, waterfalls, white-water rivers, dense forests, alpine lakes, rugged canyons. This unspoiled, breathtaking region in the northeastern corner of the state, is home to six national forests, eight national parks and state parks, the Trinity Alps, and the California Cascade range, which includes two giant glaciated volcanoes, the dormant 14,164-foot Mt. Shasta, and the still-active 10,457-foot Mt. Lassen. This California is the Wild West in the truest sense.

CENTRAL COAST

The Central Coast, with its austere cypress trees, fog-shrouded cliffs, and crashing surf immortalized in photographs by Ansel Adams and Edward Weston, continues to draw vacationers, year after year. High on a hill, the enchanting Hearst Castle lures art lovers; sheer, sculptured cliffs beckon artists; incomparable seascapes punctuated by crashing waves that capture the light call to photographers; historical monuments that pay homage to golden eras past, invite explorers. Excellent wines are created in warm inland valleys; Mediterranean-like marketplaces offer a variety of wares; and strains of Bach and Mozart float through balmy, blue skies. All of this and much more can be found along the shoreline and in the sun-washed valleys of California's enchanted Central Coast.

◄ | The weathered cypress, pounding surf, rocky beaches, sheer cliffs, birds and romping sea animals make the Monterey Peninsula one of the most memorable shorelines along the Pacific Coast.

DESERTS

Miles of sand and cactus suddenly come alive in an explosion of color; the warm desert in bloom is unforgettable. But most of the year the vast expanses of cholla, prickly pear, and Joshua trees create a desolate grandeur. Morning in the clear desert air finds jackrabbits scurrying for shelter from the day's heat; in the evening, the setting sun turns the surrounding mountain peaks from gold to magenta. California's seemingly barren deserts support a wide variety of flora and fauna and a wide range of visitor activities, from rock hunting in the hills to wind surfing on manmade lakes to camping under skies bright with stars. World-class resorts and spas encourage tennis, golf, and poolside sunning; while national parks and monuments preserve thousands of acres of nature's untouched beauty for all to enjoy.

CENTRAL VALLEY

Located between the coastal hills and the Sierra Nevada, the 18,000-square-mile Central Valley extends nearly 500 miles from the upper Sacramento Valley to the oil and cotton fields of Bakersfield. It is acre for acre, the richest agricultural region in the world. Recreation also is plentiful in this sunny valley, where lakes and rivers afford fishing, waterskiing, and picnicking. Thousands of miles of quiet waterways make for a houseboater's paradise. And historical attractions keep California's Gold Rush heritage alive. This is the California of gracious country living and enjoyment sweet as peaches in its orchards.

Joshua Tree National Monument — a true desert wonderland. This reserve demonstrates a wide range of desert environments and contains many of the species of flora and fauna typical of both the Mojave and Colorado Deserts. ▶

SAN DIEGO COUNTY

With its beautiful beaches and near-perfect climate, San Diego County epitomizes California's famous lifestyle. Forested mountains and historical sites, elegant shopping malls, ranches, and estates, farms and golf courses, a world-famous zoo and telescope are only some of the attractions that make San Diego and the surrounding communities one of California's premier vacation destinations. Set between the mountains and the sea, around one of the world's great natural harbors, the city of San Diego is, by itself, a multifaceted visitor destination. Even though it's the second largest city in California and the seventh largest in the United States, it retains a small-town charm and friendliness.

INLAND EMPIRE

Southern California's Inland Empire is a land of towering mountain peaks, fertile valleys, and vibrant communities. The region contains cities rich in culture and history and provides a wealth of recreational opportunities in the surrounding countryside. This is the land that gave rise to the popular conception that in Southern California one can water-ski and snow-ski in the same day. In the Inland Empire, it's really possible. Lakes for warm-weather sports are just a short trip from snow-clad mountains that offer a variety of winter sports. In this heart of Southern California, the visitor can explore historical sites, taste the wine of local vineyards, pick apples in season, or camp in a national forest and wilderness area only minutes away from shops and restaurants.

◄ The heritage of San Diego is reflected in the many historic landmarks of the city and in Coronado's famous seaside resort, the Hotel del Coronado.

GREATER LOS ANGELES

Los Angeles County is 4,083 square miles filled with an infinite variety of recreational and cultural opportunities. Billed as the "Entertainment Capital of the World", the region features the best in theater and music, art and museums, television and motion pictures, sporting events and world-famous attractions. With a population of nine million people, the Greater Los Angeles area is the largest metropolitan area in California and the second largest in the country. But it's much more than a metropolis. The region encompasses beaches, mountains, ocean, and desert which, combined with year-round warmth and sunshine, provide unlimited outdoor recreation.

ORANGE COUNTY

Orange County has long been famous for its family-oriented theme parks, 42 miles of shoreline, and the citrus groves that gave the area its name. But in recent years, the region has taken on an international sophistication undreamed of 50 years ago when hawks still soared the thermals, jackrabbits roamed the scrub land, and the saltworks in the Back Bay provided inspiration to artists. Located between Los Angeles and San Diego counties, Orange County stretches from the Pacific Ocean to the wilderness of the Santa Ana mountains. With an annual rainfall of only 15 inches and an average temperature of 70 degrees, the area is graced by year-round sunshine and warm Santa Ana winds.

> The coves, caves, cliffs and beaches of California provide endless opportunities for swimming, diving, surfing, boating, exploring, lying in the sun and quiet contemplation. ▶

GOLD COUNTRY

As word of the discovery of gold in California's Sierra Nevada foothills circled the globe, argonauts from around the world descended on every nook and cranny of this once-peaceful stretch of gently rolling hills and pristine mountain wilderness. They came from Panama, Mexico, Chile, from England, France, Italy, Germany, and Spain, even from Australia, to seek their fortune. Some found it, but many more did not. The miners who came to search for gold were dubbed '49ers, in reference to the first major year of the California Gold Rush. Many of them came expecting to find nuggets the size of their fists simply lying on the ground. But mining in the Gold Country proved to be miserable drudgery, filled with disappointments and setbacks. Today, more than 100 years after the first wave of hysteria, the search for gold continues, as does the legacy of these early miners.

NORTH COAST

The North Coast is the California of rugged shores and pounding surf, of towering redwood forests and rushing streams, of verdant hills and bountiful vineyards. The region extends 400 miles from San Francisco to the Oregon border and from the Pacific Ocean 50 miles inland. Traveling north from San Francisco, the visitor first encounters the elegant cosmopolitan suburbs of Marin County, then the colorful valleys of the wine country, and finally the primeval forests and untamed shores of Sonoma, Mendocino, Humboldt, and Del Norte counties. The Golden Gate Bridge links the southern tip of Marin County with San Francisco. The towns of Marin County are suburbs of San Francisco, and each has a distinctive personality, style, history, and set of attractions all its own.

◄ The Mission Basilica San Diego de Acala was founded in San Diego by Father Junipero Serra in 1769. It was the first of 21 missions founded in California.

HIGH SIERRA

The Indians held them sacred. The pioneers and gold seekers struggled trying to cross them, some dying in their attempts. Famed naturalist John Muir devoted his life to preserving them. The great photographer Ansel Adams spent a life-time trying to capture them. Few mountains are as magnificent — and none as awe-inspiring — as the Sierra Nevada. They stretch along nearly two-thirds of the eastern border of the state, from the Cascades, north to Lake Tahoe, south past Kings Canyon, where they merge with the desert Tahachapi range. They encompass mile after mile of majestic snowcapped peaks, waterfalls, alpine lakes, meadows, and endless stands of pines, firs, and giant sequoias. Sierra's superlatives stagger the imagination — a mile-high alpine lake containing 39.75 trillion gallons of water, waterfalls dropping more than 2,400 feet, sequoias taller than 20-story buildings, pines older than the pharoahs, and the highest peak in the lower continental United States, Mt. Whitney, at 14,494 feet. But statistics alone cannot convey the magnificence of these mountains, their special place in the history of the West, the mystical feeling they create, or the number of ways there are to enjoy them.

Lake Tahoe, the 22-mile long "Jewel of the Sierra", is the center of a world famous recreational area with scenic vistas, a skiiers wonderland, rugged backcountry for wilderness exploring and posh casino-hotels for indoor entertainment. ▶

Sue Tushingham McNary

SAN FRANCISCO BAY AREA

San Francisco is one of the most photographed, filmed, painted, televised and talked about cities in the world. Yet it never fails to surpass the expectations of the millions of visitors who leave their hearts here every year. Whether the city is sparkling in sunshine or coolly shrouded in fog, a view from any one of her seven principal hills reveals good reason why San Francisco holds fascination for so many people. Take the elevator to the top of Coit Tower, on Telegraph Hill in the North Beach district, and see breathtaking beauty in all directions — majestic bridges, shining blue-green water, ships, sailboats, skyscrapers, rows of pastel Victorian houses along steep streets plied by cable cars, magnificent churches, and spacious parks. "The City", as the natives simply call it, has everything. The surrounding Bay Area adds to its appeal — San Francisco is but the crown jewel in a diadem of colorful locales that make up this very special realm of California.

ABOUT THE ARTIST

Sue Tushingham McNary has become one of Southern California's best known and most widely collected artists. Her work is available through prestigious galleries and stores from coast to coast. Sue's love of California and considerable talent have merged to make this collection of scenes of California a joy to behold. The cover and five of these paintings were created specially for this book.

◀ Cable cars and Victorian houses recall the rich past of San Francisco.

Eggs & Cheese

EGGS AND CHEESE

Strong cheeses overpower good wines and good wines overpower most egg dishes (excepting many nouvelle, Italian and other quiche dishes). For the former, use lighter cheeses if you plan on serving a good wine. Otherwise, use a lesser wine because no one will know the difference, particularly with some of the gamier goat cheeses. On the egg dishes, analyze the ingredients and make a match. For example: Johannisberg Riesling with the lightest cheese omelet; Pinot Noir with a heartier Cheddar cheese version.

Artichoke-Potato Frittata

1. Beat eggs, cream, salt and pepper until evenly blended. Stir in grated cheese.

2. In 10 or 11 inch frying pan, heat 3 tablespoons of the olive oil over medium heat. Add garlic and potatoes and cook, stirring, until potatoes are tender and slightly golden. Remove from heat.

3. Combine artichokes, sliced olives, green onion and oregano; add to potatoes and cook over medium heat for about 2 minutes.

4. Pour egg mixture over vegetables and cook without stirring until it is set about ¼ inch around outer edge. With a spatula, lift some of the egg mixture from sides of pan and let uncooked egg flow to bottom. Continue cooking until frittata is almost set (the top ⅛ inch will still be liquid).

5. Invert a large round flat plate (a little larger than frying pan) over frying pan. Holding the two together, turn frittata onto plate. Add 1 remaining tablespoon of olive oil to frying pan and slide frittata back into pan. Cook about 2 minutes longer to lightly brown the bottom. Then invert onto a serving plate and cut into wedges. Yield: 4 servings.

6 eggs
2 tablespoons whipping cream or half and half
½ teaspoon salt
pepper to taste
¼ cup freshly grated Parmesan or Romano cheese
4 tablespoons olive oil
2 cloves garlic, minced
4 small red potatoes, diced
2 (8½ ounce) cans artichoke hearts, thoroughly drained
¼ cup sliced black olives
¼ cup sliced green onions, including part of tops
2 teaspoons fresh chopped oregano leaves (¼ teaspoon dried crumbled)

Note: An alternate method of browning both sides of the frittata is to put the frying pan under the broiler for a few minutes to lightly brown the top, watching carefully so as not to burn. Serve hot or at room temperature.

California Onion Tart

1 (9 inch) pie shell
3 cups thinly sliced white
  onions
3 tablespoons butter or
  bacon fat
2 cups sour cream
2 eggs, slightly beaten
¾ teaspoon salt
¼ teaspoon pepper
⅛ teaspoon nutmeg
⅛ teaspoon ground ginger
  paprika

1. Prepare a pie shell for baking using your favorite recipe. Prick bottom of pie shell and bake at 400° for 5 minutes. Remove and set aside.

2. Saute onions in butter slowly until soft and slightly golden.

3. Combine onions with sour cream, beaten eggs and spices, except paprika. Pour mixture into partially baked pie shell.

4. Bake in preheated 450° oven for 10 minutes, reduce heat to 350° and continue baking for 30 minutes or until knife blade comes out clean. Let cool for 10 to 15 minutes before cutting.

5. Sprinkle with paprika before cutting. Yield: 6 to 8 servings.

Crustless Vegetable Quiche

2 cups coarsely chopped
  mushrooms
⅔ cup chopped onions
⅔ cup chopped green
  pepper
1 cup chopped zucchini
1 teaspoon crushed garlic
  clove
2 tablespoons vegetable
  oil
5 eggs, beaten
½ cup cream
  salt and pepper to taste
1 (8 ounce) package
  cream cheese, cubed
1½ cups shredded Cheddar
  cheese
1½ cups bread croutons

1. Saute the mushrooms, onions, green pepper, zucchini and garlic in oil until tender.

2. Mix together the eggs, cream, salt and pepper and add the vegetable mixture.

3. Fold in the cubed cream cheese, Cheddar cheese and croutons and pour into a greased 9x13 inch casserole. Bake at 350° for 40 minutes. Yield: 10 to 12 servings.

Summer Quiche

1. Prepare and bake a pie shell using your favorite recipe. Cool and set aside.

2. In food processor, blend well the cottage cheese, egg yolks, lemon juice, salt and pepper. Set aside.

3. Saute the onion and garlic in oil. Let cool. Put the onion-garlic mixture in the pie crust. Cover with tomato slices and sprinkle with thyme and basil, then Gruyere cheese.

3. Beat the egg whites until stiff and fold into cottage cheese mixture. Pour over the tomato-cheese in pie shell. Smooth top with spatula and bake at 350° for 30 minutes until puffed and golden. Can be garnished with chopped basil or parsley. Yield: 6 to 8 servings.

1 **(9 inch) pie shell**
1 **cup lowfat (2%) cottage cheese**
3 **eggs, separated**
¼ **cup lemon juice**
1 **teaspoon salt**
½ **teaspoon white pepper**
1 **large onion, sliced**
1 **clove garlic, minced**
1-2 **tablespoons oil**
1 **teaspoon thyme**
1 **teaspoon basil**
1 **large tomato, thinly sliced**
¼ **cup grated Gruyere cheese**
chopped parsley or basil for garnish (optional)

◊ Nutritional information per serving:

Calories 224	Fat .... 13 g	Iron .... 2 mg
Protein .... 11 g	Cholesterol .... 88 mg	Potassium .... 201 mg
Carbohydrates .... 16 g	Calcium .... 133 mg	Sodium .... 616 mg

Tostada Quiche

1 (9 inch) deep dish pastry shell
2 avocados, peeled, seeded and mashed
1 minced garlic clove
3 tablespoons lemon juice
1 tomato, peeled, seeded and chopped
1 (4 ounce) can chopped green chiles
¼ teaspoon hot pepper sauce
8 ounces lean ground beef
¼ cup chopped onion
1-2 tablespoons taco seasoning mix
6 ounces (1½ cups) shredded Cheddar cheese
3 eggs, slightly beaten
1½ cups milk or half and half
¼ teaspoon salt
⅛ teaspoon pepper
2 cups shredded lettuce

1. Preheat oven to 400°. Prepare pastry shell using your favorite recipe; do not prick bottom of shell. Bake shell 4 to 7 minutes. Remove from oven and set aside (if bubbles form, press out while pastry is still hot).

2. Combine avocados, garlic and lemon juice. Stir in chopped tomato, 1 tablespoon of the green chiles and hot pepper sauce. Cover and refrigerate until serving time.

3. In medium skillet, combine beef, onion, remaining chiles and taco seasoning mix. Cook over medium high heat, stirring occasionally until beef is browned and onion is tender. Drain all fat.

4. Layer Cheddar cheese and then beef mixture in pastry shell. In a medium bowl or food processor combine eggs, milk, salt and pepper. Beat only until blended. Pour mixture into pastry shell. Bake at 375° for 45 minutes or until knife inserted 2 inches off-center comes out clean. Let stand for 10 minutes before serving.

5. Mix shredded lettuce with the avocado-tomato mixture and spread over top of quiche. Yield: 6 to 8 servings.

Alternate Method: Prepare quiche as directed through step 4. Place the following items in individual serving bowls and allow guests to add their own toppings: shredded lettuce, avocado-tomato mixture, corn chips, chopped tomato and black olives.

Baked Eggs in Zucchini Nests

1. Combine grated zucchini and salt in large bowl and let stand 1 hour. Squeeze excess moisture from zucchini.

2. Melt butter with olive oil in large skillet. Saute zucchini over medium heat for 1 minute or just until heated Cool.

3. Line 6 ramekins with zucchini, leaving large enough indentation for one raw egg. Dust with pepper. Drop 1 egg into each ramekin and place on baking sheet. Bake at 325° for 20 minutes or until white is set.

4. Mix egg yolks in blender for 30 seconds at medium speed. Mix in lemon juice for 10 seconds at medium speed. At high speed, very slowly in a steady stream, pour in melted butter. Top each zucchini ramekin with heaping tablespoon of sauce and serve. Yield: 6 servings.

4 pounds zucchini, grated
1 tablespoon salt
2 tablespoons butter
2 tablespoons olive oil
½ teaspoon ground pepper
6 eggs
3 egg yolks
juice of 1 lemon
½ cup butter

Mexican Spoon Bread

1. Mix together corn, milk, oil and eggs. Add corn meal, baking soda and salt.

2. Pour half the batter into greased 9x9 inch baking pan. Sprinkle with green chiles and half of the cheese. Spread remaining batter on top and sprinkle with remaining cheese.

3. Bake 45 minutes at 400°. Cool just enough to set, about 5 to 10 minutes, before cutting into serving sized squares. Yield: 8 to 10 servings.

1 (1 pound) can cream-style corn
¾ cup milk
⅓ cup vegetable oil
2 eggs, slightly beaten
1 cup corn meal
½ teaspoon baking soda
1 teaspoon salt
1½ cups shredded Cheddar cheese
1 (4 ounce) can chopped green chiles

Torta Rustica

1 (13½ ounce) package
   hot roll mix
¾ pound mild Italian
   sausage
¼ cup finely chopped
   parsley
2 tablespoons grated
   Parmesan cheese
3 small tomatoes, thinly
   sliced
4 ounces (1 cup) shredded
   mozzarella cheese
1 egg, slightly beaten

1. Prepare hot roll mix according to directions on package; set aside to rise.

2. While dough is rising, prepare filling. Remove casings from sausage and cook in a large skillet over medium heat until browned. Remove from heat, drain and discard fat. Blend meat with parsley and Parmesan.

3. Divide risen dough in half. Roll one half to fit the bottom of a greased 9x1½ inch spring-form pan. Cover dough with filling, top with tomatoes, then mozzarella. Roll remaining dough into a 9 inch square and cut into 1 inch wide strips; weave strips over dough in a lattice pattern, tucking ends of dough around filling inside pan rim. Or, for an easier method: Roll dough into a 9 inch round, cut into 8 wedges and arrange wedges side by side on top of filling with tips meeting in center.

4. Cover lightly and let rise in a warm place for about 30 to 40 minutes, until puffy looking. Uncover and gently brush top with beaten egg. Bake on lowest rack at 400° for 35 to 40 minutes. Cool on wire rack for 5 minutes.

5. Remove pan rim. Cut into wedges to serve, either warm or room temperature. Yield: 6 to 8 servings.

1. Combine all ingredients until well blended. Follow previous instructions, bake the full 40 minutes.

Alternate Filling Recipe:
- **5 ounces (½ of a package) frozen, chopped spinach, thawed, squeezed dry**
- **1 cup ricotta cheese**
- **½ cup grated Parmesan cheese**
- **1 egg yolk**
- **½ teaspoon garlic salt**
- **⅛ teaspoon pepper**

Breakfast Pie

1. Fry bacon until crisp, drain and crumble; set aside, reserving 1 tablespoon of the bacon drippings. Mix corn flake crumbs with warm bacon drippings and set aside.

2. In medium sized bowl, beat eggs until foamy. Stir in potatoes, cheeses, milk, onion, salt, pepper and hot pepper sauce. Pour into greased 9 inch pie pan and sprinkle with crumb mixture and bacon. Cover. Refrigerate overnight.

3. Bake, uncovered, at 325° for 50 minutes, or until knife comes out clean when inserted in center. Yield: 6 servings.

- **8 slices bacon**
- **½ cup corn flake crumbs**
- **5 eggs**
- **2½ cups frozen hash brown potatoes**
- **1½ cups shredded Swiss cheese**
- **½ cup cottage cheese**
- **⅓ cup milk**
- **3 green onions, thinly sliced**
- **1 teaspoon salt**
- **⅛ teaspoon pepper**
- **4 drops hot pepper sauce**

Note: Recipe can be doubled and baked in a 9x13 inch pan.

Chile Relleno Bake

1 (27 ounce) can whole green chiles
½ pound Monterey Jack cheese, grated
½ pound mild Cheddar cheese, grated
1 (28 ounce) can salsa
1 bunch green onions, chopped
4 eggs, separated
1½ cups light cream
4 tablespoons flour
½ teaspoon salt
pepper to taste
chopped cilantro (optional)

1. Split chiles, remove seeds, fill with Jack cheese. Butter a 9x13 inch casserole and arrange chiles, then cover with grated Cheddar, salsa and chopped onions.

2. Beat egg whites until foamy, add lightly beaten egg yolks, cream, flour, salt and pepper. Pour egg mixture over the chiles. Bake at 425° for 15 minutes. Lower oven temperature to 325° and continue baking for 20 to 30 minutes, or until a knife inserted into the center comes out clean.

3. Can be served hot or at room temperature. Cover with optional cilantro before serving. Yield: 8 servings.

Note: Can be prepared a day ahead, but mix the egg whites and yolks together and pour over just before baking.

California Grilled Cheese Sandwiches

1 cup shredded sharp Cheddar cheese
1 cup shredded Monterey Jack cheese
½ cup diced tomatoes
¼ cup sliced green onions
¼ teaspoon dill weed
½ teaspoon caraway seed
8 whole wheat or rye bread slices
butter or margarine, softened

1. In a medium-sized bowl, combine the cheeses, tomatoes, green onions, dill weed and caraway seed. Place cheese mixture on slices of bread; top with another slice of bread.

2. Butter the outsides of the sandwich and grill over medium heat in a large frying pan or griddle until both sides are golden brown and cheese is melted. Serve immediately. Yield: 4 servings.

Rice, Pasta & Grains

PASTA AND RICE

Young, fresh wines go best with pasta and sauces of all types. Some ideas include:

Alfredo — A great range of opportunities, from dry Chenin Blanc, to lighter Sauvignon Blanc, Pinot Blanc, Barbera and Pinot Noir.
Clam sauce — Chenin Blanc or Johannisberg Riesling.
Marinara — A big, young red, such as Barbera, Zinfandel and, perhaps, Petite Sirah.
Pesto — The best Sauvignon Blanc, or a mid-range Chardonnay.

Rice and Vegetables

1. Bring broth to boil, add rice. Stir and cover. Cook over low heat for 20 minutes.

2. Meanwhile, melt 4 tablespoons butter in skillet. Add shallots and cook until soft. Add mushrooms and cook 4 to 5 minutes longer. Add chopped broccoli and continue cooking until crispy-tender (not soft).

3. Add cooked rice to vegetables and mix. Season to taste, top with almonds. Yield: 4 servings.

1 (10¾ ounce) can chicken broth
½ cup rice
4 tablespoons butter
4 sliced shallots or ¼ cup sliced onions
½ pound sliced mushrooms
1-2 cups chopped broccoli
¼ cup sliced almonds
salt and pepper

Alternatives: Substitute julienned carrots and peas for broccoli and omit almonds; or substitute fresh chopped spinach and dill.

◊ Nutritional information per serving:

Calories 262	Fat .... 15 g	Iron .... 2 mg
Protein .... 7 g	Cholesterol .... 31 mg	Potassium .... 484 mg
Carbohydrates .... 26 g	Calcium .... 50 mg	Sodium .... 353 mg

California Rice Casserole

1. Saute onion in a large frying pan with butter for 5 minutes. Remove from heat. Stir in cooked rice, sour cream, cottage cheese, salt, pepper, green chiles and olives.

2. Put half of rice mixture in buttered 9x13 inch baking dish. Top with 1 cup of Cheddar cheese. Repeat. Bake at 375°, uncovered, for 25 to 30 minutes. Yield: 6 to 8 servings.

1 cup chopped onion
¼ cup butter
4 cups rice, cooked and cooled
1 cup sour cream
1 cup cottage cheese
½ teaspoon salt
⅛ teaspoon pepper
1 (4 ounce) can chopped green chiles
1 (4 ounce) can chopped black olives
2 cups shredded Cheddar cheese

Note: Can be made ahead. Bring to room temperature before baking.

Italian Rice Torta

⅓ cup olive oil
¼ cup finely chopped
   onion
2 tablespoons minced
   garlic
   salt and pepper to taste
2 teaspoons oregano
2 cubes chicken bouillon,
   crushed (optional)
2 tablespoons finely
   chopped parsley
4 eggs
1 cup grated Parmesan
   cheese
4 cups rice, cooked and
   cooled
4 tablespoons grated
   Monterey Jack cheese

1. Mix olive oil, onion, garlic, seasonings, eggs and Parmesan cheese together. Add cooled, well-drained rice. Mix well. Place in buttered 9x13 inch baking dish. Top with grated Monterey Jack cheese.

2. Bake for 45 minutes to 1 hour at 350°. Cut into squares and serve hot or cold. Yield: 6 to 8 servings.

Lemon Rice

1 cup uncooked white rice
1½ cups boiling water or
   chicken broth
   salt to taste
¼ cup butter
½ lemon, juice and peel
½ cup whipping cream

1. Add rice to boiling water or broth. Add salt. Cook, covered, over medium heat until done, 20 to 22 minutes.

2. Saute large pieces of lemon peel in butter for 3 minutes. Remove peel. Add butter to cooked rice. Gently toss in lemon juice, adding more to taste.

3. Warm the whipping cream and gently fold half of the cream into the rice. Add just enough of the remaining cream to coat all grains of rice. Garnish with a long strip of lemon peel, loosely tied in a knot.

4. If recipe is doubled, do not double the amount of cream. Yield: 4 to 6 servings.

Risotto with Baby Artichokes and Peas

1. Bring broth to simmer in saucepan.

2. In another large, heavy 8 quart saucepan over moderate heat, saute garlic in butter and oil; do not brown. Add rice and stir to coat well. Add wine and stir until it is absorbed.

3. Begin to add the hot broth, ½ cup at a time, stirring frequently, until each addition of broth is absorbed. This takes approximately 17 to 18 minutes. By this time most of the broth will have been added and the rice will be al dente.

4. Add artichoke and pea recipe and half of the Parmesan cheese. Stir in last of broth and season to taste. Serve at once. Pass extra cheese at the table. Yield: 6 to 8 servings.

10 **cups beef broth, pref-erably homemade**
1 **clove garlic, minced**
4 **tablespoons unsalted butter**
4 **tablespoons olive oil**
1 **clove garlic, minced**
3 **cups uncooked Arborio rice (short-grain Italian), found in Italian markets or specialty stores; regular white rice may be used**
¾ **cup dry white wine**
1 **recipe Braised Baby Artichokes and Peas (see Vegetable chapter)**
1 **cup grated Parmesan cheese**

Hunza Rice

1. Bring water or broth to boil in saucepan; add rice and simmer, cov-ered, over low heat until tender, 20 to 25 minutes.

2. In small frying pan saute onion in olive oil, covered, over low heat until softened. Chop ⅓ cup almonds in half. If using apricots, chop coarsely. Add to onions. Add to cooked rice. Yield: 4 servings.

1½ **cups water or chicken broth**
1 **cup basmati brown rice (may substitute regular brown rice)**
1 **medium red onion**
2 **tablespoons olive oil**
⅓ **cup raw California almonds**
¼ **cup California raisins or dried apricots**

◊ Nutritional information per serving:

Calories 343	Fat .... 2 g	Iron .... 2 mg
Protein .... 7 g	Cholesterol .... 0 mg	Potassium .... 300 mg
Carbohydrates .... 48 g	Calcium .... 60 mg	Sodium .... 564 mg

Risotto Milanese

2 tablespoons olive oil

2 tablespoons butter

3 cups Arborio rice (short-grain Italian rice, available in Italian markets or specialty stores); regular white rice may be used

1 onion, chopped; or 3 shallots, chopped

1 cup white wine

10 cups chicken or beef broth, preferably home-made

½-1 teaspoon saffron

¾ cup grated Parmesan cheese

½ cup chopped parsley

1. Saute onion in oil and butter 3 to 4 minutes until translucent. Add rice and cook over medium heat 2 to 3 minutes until rice is well coated.

2. In separate pan, heat broth to boiling.

3. Add wine to rice and onion mixture and cook over medium heat until absorbed. Continue to add the hot broth ½ cup at a time, stirring after each addition, and cooking until broth is absorbed. This process should take about 16 to 17 minutes, and rice should be al dente (tender, but with a slight crunch to the bite).

4. At this point, add the cheese, 1 cup more of broth (most of it should be used at this point), saffron, and parsley. The consistency of the risotto should be creamy and soupy, for it will keep cooking as it is served. Yield: 8 servings.

Optional: Serve dried red pepper flakes at the table.

Note: Good served with Osso Bucco (Braised Veal Shanks) — see Meat section.

Spaghetti Frittata

1. Beat eggs, cheese, salt and pepper in bowl.

2. In skillet, heat oil and butter. Add pasta and basil and cook over medium heat until pasta is thoroughly warmed. Add pasta to egg mixture and mix well.

3. Add pasta-egg mixture to hot skillet and cook for 7 to 8 minutes until frittata is lightly golden. Put a plate over top of frittata and invert the frittata onto the plate, then quickly slide back into skillet to cook other side for 4 minutes longer. Or, put skillet under preheated broiler for a few minutes until top is lightly browned.

4. Cut into wedges and serve at room temperature for an hors d'oeuvre or light lunch or supper. Yield: 4 to 6 servings.

8 **large eggs**
¾ **cup grated Parmesan cheese**
  salt and pepper to taste
2 **tablespoons olive oil**
2 **tablespoons unsalted butter**
3 **cups leftover spaghetti (with sauce)**
½ **cup fresh chopped basil or parsley**

Cheese Manicotti

1½ **cups ricotta**
 1 **cup mozzarella or Monterey Jack cheese, cubed**
⅓ **cup grated Parmesan**
 1 **whole egg, plus 1 yolk salt and pepper**
¼ **cup fresh chopped parsley**
 1 **cup chopped onion**
½ **cup chopped celery**
 1 **tablespoon butter**
 1 **tablespoon olive oil**
 1 **(28 ounce) can tomato puree**
 1 **teaspoon salt**
 1 **teaspoon sugar**
½ **teaspoon basil**
½ **teaspoon oregano**
 1 **bouquet garni (Place 3 or 4 sprigs of fresh parsley, two sprigs of fresh thyme, and 1 bay leaf in a 4x4 inch square of cheesecloth; tie into a bag. If fresh ingredients are not available, use ½ teaspoon parsley, ½ teaspoon thyme, and 1 bay leaf.)**
 2 **cups chicken broth**
⅔ **cup flour**
⅔ **cup milk**
 2 **eggs**
¼ **teaspoon salt**
 2 **tablespoons water**
⅓ **cup grated Parmesan cheese**
 3 **tablespoons butter**

1. Filling: Process in blender or food processor until smooth: ricotta, mozzarella, Parmesan, egg plus yolk, salt and pepper to taste, and parsley. Set aside (can be made one or two days ahead).

2. Sauce: Saute onion and celery in butter and oil in a large saucepan until transparent. Add tomatoes, salt, sugar, basil, oregano and bouquet garni. Cook, covered, for 25 minutes. Add chicken broth, cook for 20 minutes uncovered (can be made ahead and refrigerated or frozen).

3. Manicotti: In blender or food processor, add flour, milk, eggs, salt and water. Blend until smooth. Let stand, covered, for 1 hour. Add 2 more tablespoons water and blend. Pour batter onto medium-hot fry pan and turn quickly to spread thinly. Cook until crepe is set and slightly browned, turn and repeat on other side. Stack with waxed paper in between until ready to use. Yield: 12 crepes.

4. In a 9x13 inch casserole, pour ½ cup sauce in bottom of pan. Fill crepes with cheese filling and place seam-side down in pan. Top with ⅓ cup Parmesan and 1½ cups sauce. Dot with butter and bake 25 minutes at 375°. Heat extra sauce and serve at table. Yield: 4 entree servings; 6 first course servings.

Lasagna al Pesto

1. Cook spinach lasagna noodles al dente, drain and set aside.

2. Clean and chop spinach. Saute onion in 2 tablespoons olive oil. Remove from heat and stir in spinach.

3. Combine butter, ¼ cup of the grated Parmesan, parsley, garlic, basil, marjoram, olive oil and pine nuts or walnuts to make pesto sauce.

4. In large bowl, combine spinach, ¼ cup of the Parmesan, pesto, ricotta and sunflower seeds.

5. In 9x13 inch casserole, place one layer of noodles (5 noodles per layer), ⅓ filling, ⅓ mozzarella, then repeat two more times, ending with noodles. Top with last ¼ cup Parmesan and drizzle extra olive oil on top.

6. Cover with foil and bake at 350° for 30 to 40 minutes. Yield: 6 to 8 servings.

1 **pound fresh spinach**
1 **cup minced onion**
2 **tablespoons olive oil**
¼ **cup butter, softened**
¾ **cup grated Parmesan cheese**
½ **cup finely chopped parsley**
1 **clove garlic, crushed**
2 **tablespoons fresh basil or 1 teaspoon dried basil**
½ **teaspoon dried marjoram**
¼ **cup olive oil**
¼ **cup chopped pine nuts or walnuts**
2 **pounds ricotta cheese**
¼+ **cup sunflower seeds**
20 **fresh spinach lasagna noodles**
1 **pound mozzarella, grated**
1 **tablespoon olive oil**

Feta Roma Suprema

4 ounces crumbled feta
cheese
1 cup sour cream
⅓ cup heavy cream (can
substitute half and half)
ground pepper
12 roma tomatoes
2 cloves garlic
½ cup chopped basil
leaves
15-20 asparagus spears
6 large mushrooms
(shiitake are nice)
3 shallots, chopped
2 tablespoons olive oil
12 ounces fresh fettucine,
or dried

1. Mix the feta, sour cream and heavy cream so that mixture is like a thick, lumpy pancake batter. Add pepper to taste. Set aside.

2. Peel tomatoes (by dropping briefly in boiling water), then cut into 6 pieces each. Press garlic in a garlic press and mix with tomatoes and basil. Place in an oven-proof bowl. Place this mixture in an oven set at 150°.

3. Chop asparagus into ½ inch pieces. Parboil for 1 minute, drop immediately into ice water to stop cooking.

4. Saute shallots in olive oil. Add sliced mushrooms when shallots are nearly browned. Continue to saute for 3 to 4 minutes. Remove from heat.

5. Begin cooking the pasta so that it is al dente when the shallot/mushroom cooking is complete. Drain pasta and put in low shallow serving bowls. Top with tomato mixture, then mushrooms and shallot mixture, then drained asparagus. Top with a large dollop (5 to 6 tablespoons) of the feta mixture on each serving. Each person can then toss the pasta and sauce himself at the table before eating. Yield: 4 servings.

Linguini with Clam Sauce

1. Saute garlic in ⅓ cup olive oil in large skillet over medium heat until garlic is golden, not browned. Add vermouth carefully. Add basil, onion salt and pepper. Sprinkle flour lightly over skillet, return heat to moderate while stirring constantly until sauce is thickened.

2. Add the reserved clam juice to sauce, stirring well to blend. This may all be done in advance.

3. Cook linguine in boiling salted water until al dente. Drain.

4. Just minutes before linguine is done, add the clams and parsley to the sauce. Cook for 5 minutes Add the drained linguine and toss well. Serve immediately. Yield: 4 servings.

2 **cloves garlic, crushed**
⅓ **cup olive oil**
⅓ **cup dry white vermouth**
2 **tablespoons fresh chopped basil or 1½ teaspoons dried basil**
¼ **teaspoon onion salt dash of white pepper**
1½ **teaspoons flour**
2 **(8 ounce) cans minced clams, drained, reserving juice**
1 **pound linguine**
½ **cup fresh chopped parsley**

Macaroni and Cheese

1. Cook macaroni and drain.

2. In a saucepan, saute onion in butter until transparent. Stir in flour and cook one minute. Add milk and cook, stirring until sauce thickens. Add salt, Worcestershire sauce and cheese. Heat, stirring, until cheese melts.

3. Put sour cream into large bowl and gradually add hot sauce. Fold in macaroni. Pour into 7x11 inch casserole and sprinkle with bacon.

4. Bake at 375° for 25 to 30 minutes or until bubbly. Yield: 6 servings.

8 **ounces elbow macaroni**
1 **small onion, finely chopped**
¼ **cup butter**
¼ **cup flour**
1 **cup milk**
½ **teaspoon salt**
1 **teaspoon Worcestershire sauce**
1½ **cups grated sharp Cheddar cheese (6 ounces)**
½ **cup sour cream**
½ **pound bacon, cooked and crumbled**

Spaghetti with Shrimp and Mushrooms

1 **pound spaghetti or vermicelli**
½ **pound fresh mushrooms**
2 **tablespoons butter**
½ **cup butter**
4 **cloves garlic, chopped**
3 **sprigs fresh rosemary (3 inches long)**
1 **cube beef bouillon fresh ground pepper**
1 **pound cooked shrimp**
½ **cup grated Parmesan cheese**
½ **cup fresh chopped parsley**

1. Cook spaghetti or vermicelli to al dente.

2. While spaghetti is cooking, saute mushrooms in 2 tablespoons butter and set aside. In a large fry pan, place ¼ pound butter, garlic, rosemary, bouillon cube and pepper. Stir over low heat until bouillon is dissolved.

3. Just before pasta is done, add shrimp and mushrooms to butter and season to taste. Drain pasta and toss with shrimp/mushroom mixture. Sprinkle with Parmesan cheese and fresh chopped parsley. Yield: 6 servings.

Pasta with Fresh Broccoli and Onion Sauce

2 **pounds broccoli, flowerets only**
2 **onions, sliced**
2 **cloves garlic, minced**
2 **tablespoons anchovy paste (or 4 whole anchovies)**
1 **tablespoon dried red pepper flakes**
¾ **cup olive oil**
1 **pound pasta (penne or farfalle)**
1 **cup grated pecorino or romano cheese fresh ground black pepper to taste**
1 **cup toasted chopped walnuts (OPTIONAL)**

1. In very large saucepan, heat 6 quarts salted water to boiling. Add broccoli and cook 5 to 6 minutes. Remove to serving dish with slotted spoon, reserving liquid. Set aside or keep warm in oven set on very low heat.

2. In frying pan, saute onions, garlic, anchovy paste, and red pepper in olive oil over medium heat until onions are golden-brown and tender.

3. In the same water the broccoli was cooked in, cook the pasta al dente. Drain and return to pan. Add onions, broccoli, grated cheese, pepper to taste and optional walnuts. Toss to combine well. Put in a large serving dish or platter. Yield: 4 servings.

Pasta with Veal and Spinach Meatballs

1. Defrost and squeeze dry the spinach. Combine spinach, veal, eggs, garlic and parsley with bread crumbs, seasonings and ½ cup of Parmesan cheese. Mix well, but gently. Shape into 2 inch balls and place on a single layer on a baking sheet. Bake for 20 to 25 minutes at 400°, turning to brown evenly. (Can be made 1 to 2 days ahead, covered and refrigerated.)

2. Make Tomato Sauce: Saute onions, garlic, carrots, celery and anchovy paste in the olive oil until vegetables are softened, about 15 minutes. Add the wine and cook over medium-high heat until reduced by half. Add tomatoes, chicken broth, parsley, basil and seasonings. Bring to a boil, reduce heat and simmer for 1 hour. (Can be made ahead, refrigerated or frozen.)

3. Cook pasta. Meanwhile, heat sauce with meatballs. Adjust seasonings to taste. Drain pasta and gently stir in sauce and meatballs. Sprinkle with remaining cheese and chopped parsley. Yield: 12 servings.

2 (10 ounce) packages frozen chopped spinach
3 pounds ground veal
3 eggs
3 medium cloves garlic, minced
1 cup chopped parsley leaves
1 cup dried bread crumbs
1 teaspoon grated nutmeg
  salt and fresh ground black pepper
1 cup grated Parmesan cheese

Tomato Sauce:
2 medium onions, chopped
4 cloves garlic, minced
3 carrots, chopped
2 stalks celery, chopped
2 tablespoons anchovy paste
¾ cup olive oil
1 cup dry red or white wine
2 (28 ounce) cans crushed tomatoes with added puree
1 cup chicken broth
1 bunch fresh chopped basil (or chopped parsley and basil combination)
  salt and pepper to taste
½ teaspoon thyme
1 bay leaf
2 pounds pasta (Mostaciolli or penne or farfalle)

Spicy Spaghetti with Shellfish

2 **pounds clams, small in the shell**
1 **pound large (not jumbo) shrimp, shelled and deveined (save shells for stock)**
1 **pound scallops (if large, cut in half)**
8 **tablespoons olive oil**
3 **cloves garlic, minced**
1 **tablespoon anchovy paste**
1 **tablespoon dried red pepper**
1 **stalk celery, chopped**
1 **carrot, chopped**
1 **onion, chopped**
2 **(28 ounce) cans tomato puree**
1½ **cups white wine**
 salt to taste
½ **cup chopped parsley**
2 **pounds spaghetti**

1. Soak clams in salted water 30 minutes. Rinse thoroughly. Put in large skillet with ¾ cup of the wine and ¾ cup water. Cover and boil until clams open. Discard unopened clams. Remove with slotted spoon as they open. Remove meat from shells and set aside. Cover and refrigerate. Boil juice down until reduced by half and strain.

2. Shell and devein shrimp. Make Fish Stock: Take shells and put in saucepan with 8 cups water, onion, carrot, bay leaf, thyme, parsley, salt and pepper. Bring to boil, skim, simmer 1 hour, until reduced by half and strain.

3. Make Tomato Sauce: Saute 3 cloves garlic in 4 tablespoons olive oil with anchovy paste and red pepper. Add chopped celery, carrot, and onion and saute until tender. Add tomato puree, wine, fish stock and strained clam broth. Cook for 30 minutes, uncovered. Season to taste.

4. Cook spaghetti in salted boiling water for 4 to 5 minutes (very al dente). Drain and put in baking dish (9x13 inch) lined with a large piece of heavy-duty aluminum foil (enough to cover the bottom of the pan and fold over to form a package later). Toss with 1 or 2 cups of the sauce.

5. In large skillet, heat remaining 4 tablespoons olive oil and saute shrimp until just pink; 1 minute on each side. Remove to pasta in foil. Add scallops to skillet and saute for about 1 minute. Add parsley and remove to pasta in foil. Add reserved clams.

6. Lightly toss pasta/seafood with 3 to 4 cups additional sauce and fold foil over tightly to make a package. Bake at 375° for 10 to 12 minutes. Be careful opening the package as steam is very hot. Serve immediately, with extra heated sauce at table and extra chopped parsley to garnish. Yield: 6 to 8 servings.

Fish Stock:
shrimp shells
8 cups water
1 onion
1 carrot
1 bay leaf
thyme
parsley
salt and pepper

Note: Much of this recipe may be prepared in the morning. Cook the pasta, saute the shrimp and scallops, and bake the dish just before you serve it.

Seafood Pasta Del Mar

1. Over medium heat, in large frying pan, saute garlic in 2 tablespoons oil and 2 tablespoons butter. Add seafood and saute for 4 to 5 minutes (do not overcook). Add lemon juice, white wine, parsley and salt and pepper to taste. Saute 2 more minutes. Remove from heat, cover to keep warm.

2. Over medium heat in a large frying pan, heat 1 tablespoon oil and 1 tablespoon butter and saute carrots for 5 minutes. Add broccoli and cook for 5 minutes longer. Add zucchini and saute for 2 minutes. Add oregano and basil. Remove from heat and cover to keep warm.

3. Cook fettuccine according to package instructions (al dente). Meanwhile heat remaining 4 tablespoons butter, cream, and Parmesan cheese together. Drain pasta and toss with seafood, vegetables and cream sauce. Serve immediately. Yield: 4 to 6 servings.

3 cloves garlic, minced
3 tablespoons olive oil
7 tablespoons butter
8 ounces large shrimp, peeled and deveined
8 ounces large scallops
8 ounces crab meat
1-2 tablespoons lemon juice
2 tablespoons white wine
2 tablespoons chopped fresh parsley
salt and pepper to taste
2 carrots, sliced on the diagonal
1 cup broccoli flowerets
1 zucchini, sliced
1 teaspoon oregano
2 tablespoons chopped fresh basil
12 ounces fettuccine
4 ounces heavy cream
½ cup Parmesan cheese

Wheat-Bulgur Pilaf

2 tablespoons butter
½ cup chopped celery
1 medium onion, chopped
½ cup fresh sliced mush-
   rooms
1 cup cracked wheat
   bulgur, uncooked
¼ teaspoon dill
½ teaspoon salt
¼ teaspoon oregano
¼ teaspoon pepper
1½ cups chicken broth
½ cup dry white wine
1 tablespoon chopped
   parsley

1. Saute celery, onion and mush-rooms in butter; add bulgur. Cook until vegetables are tender and bulgur is golden-yellow. Add season-ings, broth and wine.

2. Bring to a boil; stir with fork and cover; turn heat on low and simmer for 20 minutes or until liquid is absorbed. Stir in parsley and serve. Yield: 4 servings.

◊ Nutritional information per serving:

Calories 248	Fat .... 7 g	Iron .... 3 mg
Protein .... 7 g	Cholesterol .... 16 mg	Potassium .... 313 mg
Carbohydrates .... 36 g	Calcium .... 37 mg	Sodium .... 624 mg

Barley Pilaf

1 cup pearl barley
6-8 tablespoons butter
1 medium onion, chopped
2 carrots, diced
1 tablespoon fresh pars-
   ley, chopped
2-3 green onions, sliced
½ pound fresh mush-
   rooms, sliced
2½ cups chicken broth (up
   to 3 cups may be used)
   salt and pepper to taste

1. Rinse barley with cold water, drain well.

2. Melt butter and saute onion, mushrooms and barley until barley is toasted. Remove from heat, add remaining ingredients, except for broth. Spoon into a 2 quart casserole. (Can be refrigerated at this point.)

3. Heat broth to boiling and add to barley mixture in casserole. Blend well. Bake, covered, at 375° for 70 to 90 minutes. Before serving, garnish with chopped parsley or carrot curls. Yield: 6 to 8 servings.

Seafood

SEAFOOD

One of the great combinations in gastronomy is a great California Chardonnay or Pinot Blanc with the finest Dover sole, lobster or other seafood dish with a more delicate nature. The more intense the flavor of the fish, crustacean and sauce, the more straight forward character needed in the wine and the balancing act can create interesting combinations. Examples:

Abalone — Pinot Blanc, Sauvignon Blanc, Johannisberg Riesling.

Clams — Lighter style whites so the flavor of the clams isn't overpowered.

Crab Legs — Lighter style Chardonnay, Pinot Blanc.

Halibut — As always, depends on the sauce; from Sauvignon Blanc and Chardonnay with the classic white sauces or meuniere style, to Pinot Noir with a red sauce.

Mussels — Lighter style whites.

Oysters — On the half shell, with Chardonnay or Pinot Blanc; same with Rockefeller or other subtle dishes; move to the mid-range reds with red sauces.

Salmon — Chardonnay, but also a rich Sparkling Wine.

Tuna — Sauvignon Blanc; dry Chenin Blanc; dry Gewurztraminer.

Grilled Shrimp

1. Mix together oil, lemon juice, parsley, garlic, salt, oregano and pepper in a long shallow bowl. Put shrimp on skewers and marinate for at least 2 hours.

2. Grill for 3 minutes on each side over hot coals. Serve with lemon wedges and Basil Mayonnaise (recipe in Salad Section). Don't forget finger bowls! Yield: 6 servings.

2 pounds jumbo shrimp, unshelled and deveined (plan on 3 to 4 jumbo shrimp per person)
¾ cup olive oil
2 tablespoons lemon juice
2 tablespoons minced parsley
2 cloves garlic, minced
1 teaspoon salt
½ teaspoon oregano
½ teaspoon pepper

◊ Nutritional information per serving:

Calories 392	Fat .... 20 g	Iron .... 5 mg
Protein .... 32 g	Cholesterol .... 295 mg	Potassium .... 297 mg
Carbohydrates .... 1 g	Calcium .... 68 mg	Sodium .... 695 mg

Simple Scampi

1. In oven-proof 10x14 inch baking dish, combine all ingredients; toss the shrimp until well-coated with mixture.

2. Place under broiler and broil shrimp for 4 to 5 minutes on each side, basting several times. BE CAREFUL NOT TO OVERCOOK.

3. Serve over brown or white rice. Yield: 4 to 6 servings.

1 pound large, raw shrimp, deveined and shelled
2 tablespoons lemon juice
2 green onions, finely chopped
2 tablespoons fresh, minced parsley
1 clove garlic, minced
4 tablespoons butter, melted
¼ cup olive oil
dash salt
1 (2 ounce) jar chopped pimento (optional)

Spicy Shrimp

2 **pounds shrimp, un-shelled**
3 **bay leaves**
8 **whole peppercorns**
1 **tablespoon salt**
1 **(12 ounce) can beer**
1 **dried red pepper, or 1 to 2 teaspoons dried red pepper flakes**

1. Place all ingredients in a very large saucepan. If beer doesn't cover shrimp completely, add water. Start cooking over low heat, then turn up to moderate heat, watching closely (the beer will foam) until boiling point is reached.

2. Let boil 5 to 10 minutes or until done but not overcooked. Remove cover and allow shrimp to cool slightly in cooking liquid. Drain.

3. Serve in the shells, letting each person peel their own. Serve with cocktail sauce for dipping. Yield: 2 to 4 servings.

Note: Spicy Shrimp does not freeze well and should not be prepared ahead of time. Serve immediately.

◊ Nutritional information per serving:

Calories 287	Fat ....4 g	Iron ....6 mg
Protein ....22 g	Cholesterol ....345 mg	Potassium ....492 mg
Carbohydrates ....8 g	Calcium ....148 mg	Sodium ....1942 mg

Shrimp and Fish au Gratin

1 **cup chopped celery**
2 **green onions, chopped**
2 **tablespoons olive oil**
1 **large clove garlic, chopped**
1 **cup unseasoned croutons**
½ **cup chicken broth**
6 **ounces cooked tiny shrimp**
1½ **teaspoons dill**
¼ **teaspoon white pepper**
6 **fillets of orange roughy**
4 **tablespoons lemon juice**

1. Saute celery, onion and garlic in olive oil. Add dill and pepper.

2. Add chicken broth to unseasoned croutons; gently mix together celery, onions, and garlic with croutons and add shrimp.

3. Place fish fillets in a buttered 9x12 inch glass baking dish; sprinkle with lemon juice. Spoon above mixture over fish. Bake 30 minutes at 350°. Garnish with fresh chopped parsley and lemon wedges. Yield: 6 servings.

Seafood Supreme

1. Saute onions and celery in butter until tender. Combine with crab, prawns, rice, water chestnuts, mayonnaise, lemon juice and salt. Pour into buttered 9x13 inch baking dish.

2. Seafood Supreme is tastier if it is refrigerated at this point for 24 hours. It can, however, be finished and baked immediately.

3. Sprinkle with bread crumbs and cheese. Bake at 350° for 25 to 30 minutes. Remove from oven and let stand for about 10 minutes before serving. Yield: 8 servings.

1 cup chopped onion
2 cups chopped celery
2 tablespoons butter
½ pound fresh crabmeat, shredded
1 pound prawns, cooked and cut-up
2½ cups rice, cooked
½ cup water chestnuts, sliced
1 cup mayonnaise
3 tablespoons lemon juice
½ teaspoon salt or to taste
1 cup Monterey Jack or mild Cheddar cheese, grated
1 cup fine seasoned bread crumbs

Crab and Shrimp Baked with Artichoke Hearts

1. Grease a 2 quart baking dish and arrange artichoke hearts, crab meat and shrimp. Saute mushrooms for 4 to 5 minutes in 2 tablespoons of the butter and add to dish.

2. Melt remaining 2 teaspoons of butter in saucepan and stir in flour, salt, pepper and cayenne pepper. Add whipping cream and stir until smooth. Add Worcestershire sauce and sherry.

3. Pour sauce over crab-shrimp mixture and sprinkle with Parmesan cheese. Bake at 375° for 30 minutes.

4. Serve over bed of cooked white rice, and garnish with chopped fresh parsley and lemon wedges. Yield: 4 to 6 servings.

1 (8½ ounce) can artichoke hearts, drained (not marinated)
½ pound fresh crab meat
½ pound fresh shrimp, cooked, peeled and deveined
½ pound mushrooms, sliced
2 tablespoons plus 2 teaspoons butter
2½ tablespoons flour
½ teaspoon salt
¼ teaspoon pepper
dash cayenne pepper
1 cup whipping cream
1 tablespoon Worcestershire sauce
2 tablespoons dry sherry
½ cup grated Parmesan cheese

Pismo Beach Baked Clams

1 **large onion, minced**
4 **tablespoons minced parsley**
2 **tablespoons olive oil**
2 **tablespoons butter**
1 **pound clams, chopped**
2 **slices bacon, fried crisp, crumbled**
6 **slices bread**
   salt and pepper to taste
   milk
1 **(8 ounce) can tomato sauce**
½ **cup buttered soda crackers, crumbled to crumbs**
½ **cup grated Parmesan cheese**

1. Soak bread in milk and squeeze dry; crumble.

2. Brown onion and parsley in oil and butter. Add clams, bacon and bread. Salt and pepper to taste, then add tomato sauce.

3. Divide mixture among 6 or 8 buttered shells or ramekins, topping each with a sprinkling of cracker crumbs.

4. Bake 30 minutes at 350°. Sprinkle with grated cheese before serving. Yield: 6 to 8 servings.

Crab Meat in Shell Dishes

2 **cups soft white bread pieces, crust removed**
½ **cup milk**
2 **cups fresh crab meat, broken into small pieces**
6 **eggs, hard boiled, chopped**
½ **onion, grated**
2 **tablespoons chopped fresh parsley**
½ **cup mayonnaise (more may be added if needed)**
1-2 **teaspoons salt**
½ **teaspoon pepper**
½ **cup cracker crumbs**
1 **tablespoon butter**
   olives stuffed with pimento, for garnish

1. Pour milk over bread and set aside.

2. Gently combine crab meat, eggs, onion, mayonnaise, parsley, salt and pepper. Drain excess milk that bread has not absorbed and carefully fold bread into crab meat mixture.

3. Lightly butter 8 individual baking shells or 6 inch baking dishes and pile with crab mixture. Melt butter and stir into cracker crumbs. Sprinkle on top of crab.

4. Bake 20 to 30 minutes at 325°, until crumbs are brown and crisp. Garnish with slice of pimento olive. Yield: 8 servings.

Monterey Crab Enchiladas

1. Heat tortillas one at a time in hot oil until soft. Place ¼ cup crab meat in center of each tortilla and sprinkle with 1 tablespoon onion. Spread with a little Salsa con Tomatillos, roll up and place seam side down in 8x11 inch baking dish. Cover with remaining salsa. Sprinkle with cheese.

2. Bake at 400° for 10 minutes until hot and cheese is melted. Serve with Sour Cream Sauce. Yield: 4 to 6 servings.

1. Remove paper husks from tomatillos; cover with water and cook until tender, about 15 minutes. Drain off half of the liquid and blend in blender. Heat ¼ cup oil in pan and cook onions, chiles, and garlic until soft. Add cilantro and salt, then add to tomatillos in blender. Fry tortillas in oil until softened and add to blender. If too thick add a little water.

1. Mash garlic with salt; combine with other ingredients. Add more chiles if you prefer sauce to be hotter.

6 corn tortillas
vegetable oil
1½ cups crab meat
6 tablespoons minced onion
Salsa con Tomatillos (recipe below)
shredded Monterey Jack cheese
Sour Cream Sauce (recipe below)

Salsa con Tomatillos:
2 dozen tomatillos
¼ cup vegetable oil
2 jalapeno chiles, chopped
½ cup chopped onion
2 tablespoons chopped cilantro
1 clove garlic, minced
1 teaspoon salt
2 corn tortillas

Sour Cream Sauce:
¼ teaspoon garlic, minced
½ teaspoon salt
1 cup sour cream
2 tablespoons chopped onion
2 tablespoons chopped cilantro
2 tablespoons chopped green chiles

Cioppino

1½ cups chopped onion
2 cloves garlic, chopped
½ cup chopped green
   pepper
1 cup chopped celery
¼ cup olive oil
1 (14 ounce) can tomatoes
2 (8 ounce) cans tomato
   sauce
1 teaspoon basil
1 teaspoon thyme
1 teaspoon oregano
2 teaspoons salt
½ teaspoon pepper
1 cup dry red wine
1 cup water or clam juice
¼ pound or more shelled
   shrimp, cut in half
½ pound chunk crab
1 pound firm white fish,
   cubed in 1 inch pieces
½ pound scallops
   fresh parsley, for garnish

1. Saute onion, garlic, green pepper and celery in oil until soft but not brown.

2. Add tomatoes, tomato sauce, spices, wine and water. Heat to boiling, then simmer 30 minutes. This may be done a day or two in advance, then refrigerated.

3. Add shrimp, crab, white fish and scallops to simmering sauce. Cook over medium-high heat 10 to 15 minutes. Add more tomato sauce if needed.

4. Serve in wide, shallow soup bowls garnished with fresh parsley with plenty of crusty bread for soaking up the sauce. Yield: 6 to 8 servings.

◊ Nutritional information per serving:

Calories 261	Fat .... 9 g	Iron .... 2 mg
Protein .... 30 g	Cholesterol .... 82 mg	Potassium .... 983 mg
Carbohydrates .... 11 g	Calcium .... 104 mg	Sodium .... 1231 mg

Skillet Fish Cantonese with Fresh Herbs

1. Combine water, soy sauce, lemon juice, ginger, half of scallions and red pepper, garlic and a quarter of cilantro in non-stick skillet. Bring to boil and simmer 5 minutes.

2. Add fish and top with remaining herbs, vegetables and pepper. Cover loosely and simmer for about 5 minutes or until fish is just beginning to flake.

3. Place fish on serving plate, top with vegetables and sauce. Garnish with extra cilantro and lemon wedges if desired. Yield: 2 to 3 servings.

¼ **cup water**
¾ **teaspoon soy sauce**
1 **teaspoon lemon juice**
2-3 **tablespoons finely shredded fresh ginger**
2 **scallions, finely shredded**
1-2 **tablespoons mild Anaheim chile pepper or red pepper, minced**
1 **clove garlic, minced**
½ **cup chopped cilantro pepper to taste**
1 **pound fish fillets (snapper, sea bass or halibut) lemon wedges cilantro for garnishing**

◊ Nutritional information per serving:

Calories 159	Fat ....2 g	Iron ....0.42 mg
Protein ....31 g	Cholesterol ....56 mg	Potassium ....671 mg
Carbohydrates ....1 g	Calcium ....53 mg	Sodium ....183 mg

California Seabass Casserole

1. Place sliced tomatoes in buttered casserole. Sprinkle with crumbs, salt and pepper. Arrange fillets on top.

2. In a small saucepan, combine wine, butter and lime juice. Boil 3 minutes. Pour over fish. Sprinkle with cilantro, Parmesan cheese and paprika.

3. Bake at 500° for 10 minutes per inch of thickness — or until flaky. Don't overcook. Yield: 4 servings.

2 **tomatoes, sliced**
3 **tablespoons Italian bread crumbs**
salt and pepper to taste
1½ **pounds seabass fillets**
1½ **cups dry white wine**
½ **cup butter**
2 **teaspoons lime juice**
¼ **cup fresh chopped cilantro**
¼ **cup grated Parmesan cheese**
paprika

Red Snapper Vera Cruz

2 pounds red snapper
   fillets
½ lemon
   salt and pepper
2 tablespoons vegetable
   oil
½ cup chopped onion
2 cloves garlic, minced
2-3 fresh tomatoes, diced
3 tablespoons chopped
   parsley
1 tablespoon vinegar
1 teaspoon salt
1 bay leaf
¼ teaspoon thyme
¼ teaspoon marjoram
¼ teaspoon oregano
1 teaspoon sugar (op-
   tional)
¼ cup water
8-10 stuffed green olives,
   sliced
2 teaspoons capers
   (optional)
2-4 tablespoons canned
   chopped green chiles

1. Rub fish with lemon; season with salt and pepper. Fry one minute on each side in hot oil; remove to shallow baking dish.

2. Saute onion, garlic and tomatoes in remaining oil for 5 minutes. Add parsley, vinegar, salt, bay leaf, thyme, marjoram, oregano, sugar and water; cook 2 minutes longer.

3. Top fish with olives, capers and chiles. Pour sauce over all. Bake at 325° for 15 to 20 minutes, or until fish flakes apart when tested. Yield: 4 servings.

◊ Nutritional information per serving:

Calories 230	Fat .... 8 g	Iron .... 1 mg
Protein .... 32 g	Cholesterol .... 56 mg	Potassium .... 844 mg
Carbohydrates .... 6 g	Calcium .... 74 mg	Sodium .... 749 mg

Stuffed Yellowtail

1. Rinse and dry inside of fish. Season inside with salt and pepper. Set aside.

2. Saute garlic, onion, celery in butter until crisp-tender, but not brown. Add mushrooms, saute 3 minutes longer. Add zucchini, parsley, bread crumbs, oregano, and salt and pepper to taste.

3. Stuff fish. Place uncooked bacon over top of fish. Bake at 400° 10 minutes for each 1 inch of stuffed thickness. Yield: 10 to 12 servings.

1 **whole yellowtail or albacore (about 6 pounds)**
   salt and pepper
3 **cloves garlic, minced**
½ **cup chopped onion**
½ **cup chopped celery**
3 **tablespoons butter**
1 **cup sliced mushrooms**
1 **medium zucchini, diced**
½ **cup parsley, chopped**
2-3 **cups fresh bread crumbs**
1 **teaspoon oregano**
6-8 **slices bacon**

Sole Florentine

1. Cook spinach and drain well.

2. Blend sour cream with flour, onions, lemon juice and salt. Combine half of this mixture with the spinach.

3. Spread spinach evenly over bottom of a shallow baking dish (9x13 inch or 10x15 inch). Place sole fillets over spinach and dot with butter. Spread remaining sour cream mixture over sole and dust lightly with paprika.

4. Bake at 375° for 25 minutes or until fish flakes when tested with a fork. Yield: 6 to 8 servings.

3 **(10 ounce) packages frozen chopped spinach**
2 **cups sour cream**
3 **tablespoons flour**
½ **cup finely chopped green onions**
   juice of one lemon
2 **teaspoons salt**
1½ **pounds thin sole fillets**
2 **tablespoons butter**
   paprika

Salmon en Croute

1 **pound salmon**
¾ **cup white wine**
¾ **cup water**
3 **(10 ounce) packages frozen chopped spinach, thawed and drained**
3 **tablespoons minced chives**
1 **teaspoon salt**
¼ **teaspoon pepper**
¼ **teaspoon nutmeg**
¼ **cup butter**
¼ **cup minced onion**
1 **pound fresh mushrooms, thinly sliced**
2 **tablespoons lemon juice**
½ **teaspoon salt**
¼ **teaspoon pepper**
1 **sheet puff pastry**
½ **pound thin Swiss cheese slices**
1 **egg yolk**
lemon wedges for garnishing
parsley for garnishing

1. Poach salmon in wine and water until tender (about 10 minutes if 1 inch thick).

2. Preheat oven to 425°. Combine spinach, chives, salt, pepper and nutmeg in a bowl. Set aside.

3. Melt butter in frying pan and saute onion until golden. Add mushrooms, lemon juice, salt and pepper and cook until mushrooms are soft and all liquid has evaporated.

4. Roll sheet of puff pastry into a 12x14 inch rectangle. Lay half of the Swiss cheese slices down the length of the pastry, leaving a 1 inch border at each end. Spread mushroom layer (drain off any excess liquid) on top of the cheese.

5. Place poached salmon pieces on top of mushroom layer. Top with spinach mixture, then remaining cheese slices.

6. Fold sides of pastry over middle, press together to seal. Roll pastry over onto brown paper, sealed side down. Shape pastry into an even shape; tuck ends under and seal.

7. Beat 1 egg yolk with 1 tablespoon water and brush entire pastry surface with egg mixture. Cut out some pastry strips, leaves or flowers, place on loaf, brush with more egg mixture.

8. Make two (½ inch) slits at each end of loaf. Bake 20 minutes at 425°

9. Reduce heat to 375° and bake 30 minutes longer. Cool 10 minutes: then serve. Garnish with lemon wedges and parsley. Yield: 6 to 8 servings.

Broiled Salmon in Teriyaki Marinade

1. Combine soy sauce, sugar, mustard, garlic powder, parsley, ginger and wine to make teriyaki marinade.

2. Pour over salmon and allow to marinate for at least 6 hours.

3. Combine butter with garlic powder, oregano and rosemary. Broil salmon 4 inches from heat for 5 to 7 minutes or until done, basting with butter mixture. Do not overcook. Garnish with sesame seeds. Yield: 12 servings.

1 **cup soy sauce**
4½ **ounces brown sugar**
¼ **teaspoon dry mustard**
¾ **teaspoon garlic powder**
2 **tablespoons chopped fresh parsley**
1 **teaspoon fresh chopped ginger**
1 **ounce white wine**
4-5 **pound salmon fillet, cut into 5 to 6 ounce portions**
1½ **cups butter, softened**
2 **teaspoons garlic powder**
2 **teaspoons oregano, crumbled**
1 **teaspoon dried rosemary, ground**
toasted sesame seeds for garnish

Baked Fish Aegean

1. Rinse fish and dry with paper towels. Mix olive oil with chopped garlic cloves.

2. Place a small amount of the oil in the bottom of an 8x10 inch baking pan. Spread fish over bottom of pan and sprinkle with the lemon juice. Top with onions, seasonings, parsley, tomatoes, the remaining oil, and the bread crumbs.

3. Bake for 1 hour at 350°. If top color is desired, broil after baking. Let sit for 15 minutes before serving. Yield: 4 servings.

1½ **pounds fish (halibut, orange roughy, sea bass, snapper or salmon)**
½ **cup olive oil**
1-2 **garlic cloves, finely chopped**
juice of 1 lemon
4 **green onions, cut in half and split**
1 **Bermuda onion, sliced**
½ **teaspoon oregano**
¼ **teaspoon salt**
¼ **teaspoon pepper**
¼ **cup chopped parsley**
1 **(1 pound 13 ounce) can tomatoes with juice, chopped**
½ **cup bread crumbs**

Salmon in Hollandaise Sauce

½ **pound mushrooms, finely chopped**
1 **medium onion, finely chopped**
1 **tablespoon parsley, finely chopped**
3 **tablespoons butter**
2 **cups Hollandaise Sauce (see below)**
6 **1½ inch thick salmon steaks**
3 **cups dry white wine**

1. Saute mushrooms, onion and parsley in butter until golden brown. Blend mixture into Hollandaise Sauce; whip gently until well-mixed. Chill sauce until firm.

2. Place salmon steaks in a large skillet and cover with wine. Cover and poach gently until fish is bright pink and wine has been reduced to below the salmon level. Remove salmon; place in baking dish. Cover each piece of salmon with a generous spread of the firmed sauce.

3. Move oven rack down to second level in oven and broil fish for 5 minutes, until sauce becomes glazed and golden brown. Serve on hot platter with poaching wine poured around the fish. Yield: 6 servings.

Hollandaise Sauce:
½ **cup butter**
3 **egg yolks, lightly beaten**
2½ **teaspoons fresh lemon juice**
¼ **teaspoon salt**
pinch cayenne pepper

1. Melt butter in 1½ quart saucepan.

2. Place egg yolks, lemon juice, salt and cayenne in a blender; turn blender on and off once quickly. Turn the blender on high, remove the lid, and slowly pour the butter in, forming a steady stream.

3. Turn the blender off, remove sauce and pour into a bowl. Serve warm. If it begins to cool before serving, warm in a shallow pan of warm water. Yield: 1 cup.

Seafood Sausage with Fennel Sauce

1. In a heavy skillet, saute onions, fennel and garlic in ¼ cup butter until tender, but not browned. Set aside. In food processor fitted with steel blade, coarsely chop fish, shrimp and scallops. Add tomato and process, using on and off pulse until small chunks are visible. Do not puree until smooth. Remove from work bowl to a medium sized mixing bowl. Add egg, cream, seasonings, and the sauteed onion-fennel mixture. Stir to combine.

2. Rinse sausage casings inside and out carefully, to remove all salt. Pat dry. Following manufacturer's instructions, stuff seafood sausage mixture into casings. Twist or tie ends with string, making sausage into 4 inch links. Refrigerate until ready to cook (up to 3 to 4 hours ahead).

3. Preheat oven to 350°. Make Fennel Sauce (recipe follows). Just before serving, heat 2 tablespoons butter in heavy skillet. Carefully brown sausage links, turning to brown all sides. Set on paper towel to absorb any extra butter. Place sausage on heavy jelly-roll pan or shallow baking dish and bake 10 minutes. Do not overbake.

4. If sauce has cooled, re-heat in double boiler. Spoon one small ladle of sauce over a sausage link on small individual plates (for appetizer); garnish with a sprig of fennel or watercress on top. Use two or more links for a main course. Yield: 12 appetizers or 4 to 6 main course servings.

¼ **cup finely chopped onions**
⅓ **cup finely chopped fennel bulb**
1 **clove garlic, minced**
¼ **cup butter**
¾ **pound red snapper, boned**
¾ **pound orange roughy, boned**
⅓ **pound bay shrimp, cleaned**
10 **large scallops, washed**
1 **small tomato, seeded and quartered**
1 **egg, lightly beaten**
⅓ **cup heavy cream**
⅛ **teaspoon freshly grated nutmeg**
⅛ **teaspoon white pepper**
4 **feet pork sausage casings**
2 **tablespoons clarified butter**

Fennel Sauce

1 clove garlic, minced
½ cup finely minced fennel bulb
¼ cup minced green onions and tops
¼ cup butter
1 cup dry white wine (good quality)
3 tablespoons minced watercress leaves
1 tablespoon finely snipped fennel tops
2 dashes white pepper
⅛ teaspoon freshly grated nutmeg
1½ cups heavy cream
¼ cup softened butter
1 tablespoon Pernod liqueur
2-3 drops green food coloring

1. In heavy saucepan or skillet, saute garlic, fennel bulb and onions in butter until tender but not browned. Add wine, stirring occasionally. Simmer and reduce liquid volume to ¼ cup. Use a low heat and do not brown.

2. Add watercress, green onion tops and cream. Stir with whisk until smooth. Add seasonings, correcting if necessary. Simmer on very low heat 3 minutes; do not boil. Whisk in butter, 1 tablespoon at a time. Add Pernod and food coloring. Color should be very light green.

Note: Excellent served over any type of grilled or poached fish, or as a base for a terrific soup.

Poultry

POULTRY

What a selection! Imagine, Cabernet Sauvignon with turkey, duck or quail. Chardonnay with turkey, as well, and roasted chicken. Zinfandel, Barbera and Merlot with barbecue. Pinot Noir with rabbit or goose. This is an area where the great cooks of the world experiment more than any other, to the wonderment and appreciation of those fortunate enough to sample the new combinations.

Summer Chicken Breasts

1. Roast peppers.

2. Pound chicken breasts slightly between waxed paper to flatten.

3. Combine oil, lime juice, balsamic vinegar, Dijon mustard, garlic, 2 tablespoons of the cilantro, salt and pepper in a bowl and marinate chicken for at least 1 hour.

4. Grill or broil chicken breasts for 2 minutes on each side, basting once. Sprinkle with remaining cilantro and serve with roasted red or yellow peppers. Yield: 4 servings.

4 red or yellow peppers
4 chicken breasts, boned and skinned (½ pound each)
⅓ cup olive oil
2 limes, juice only
¼ cup balsamic vinegar
1 teaspoon Dijon mustard
2 cloves garlic, crushed
4 tablespoons chopped cilantro
½ teaspoon seasoned salt
½ teaspoon seasoned pepper

◊ Nutritional information per serving:

Calories 297	Fat ....15 g	Iron..........................2 mg
Protein ....34 g	Cholesterol ....87 mg	Potassium ....387 mg
Carbohydrates ....7 g	Calcium ....27 mg	Sodium ....359 mg

Tokyo Chicken with Mandarin-Raisin Sauce

1. Mix soy sauce, wine, water, sugar, ginger, scallions and garlic in greased casserole dish. Roll thighs in mixture until all pieces are well coated. Bake in same casserole dish at 375° for 20 minutes.

2. Turn and bake another 20 minutes, or until done. Remove chicken to platter.

3. Pour pan juices into saucepan, and add cornstarch-water mixture, oranges, and raisins. Cook over medium heat until glossy. Pour over chicken and serve with rice. Yield: 4 to 6 servings.

½ cup soy sauce
¼ cup white wine
¼ cup water
2 tablespoons sugar
¼ teaspoon ginger
2 medium scallions, chopped
1 clove garlic, minced
12 chicken thighs, skinned
1½ teaspoons cornstarch, mixed in 1 tablespoon cold water
1 (11 ounce) can mandarin oranges
¼ cup raisins

Mushroom-Stuffed Chicken

2 broiler-fryer chickens, halved
1 lemon
2 teaspoons salt
⅛ teaspoon pepper
½ teaspoon paprika
½ cup butter, melted
¼ cup sherry
3 tablespoons butter
½ pound mushrooms, sliced
1 tablespoon flour
1 tablespoon parsley
½ cup cream
½ teaspoon salt
⅛ teaspoon pepper

1. Place chicken halves in broiler pan with rack. Cut lemon in half and rub entire surface of chicken, squeezing so there is plenty of juice. Mix together salt, pepper and paprika and sprinkle over chicken.

2. Broil skin side down approximately 8 inches from heat for about 15 minutes, basting occasionally with butter and sherry which have been mixed together.

3. Meanwhile, in a small frying pan melt 3 tablespoons butter; add mushrooms. Cook 3 to 4 minutes until mushrooms are soft, but not browned. Stir in flour and parsley. Add cream, stirring constantly until mixture is smooth. Season with salt and pepper.

4. Turn chicken after first 15 minutes, continue to broil about 15 minutes longer, basting occasionally.

5. Remove chicken from broiler pan and place in baking dish, skin side down. Fill chicken cavities with mushroom stuffing and bake at 375° for about 15 minutes or until chicken is done. Yield: 4 to 6 servings.

Rye Chicken Casserole

1. Sprinkle chicken pieces with salt and pepper. Heat butter and oil in oven-proof pan, brown chicken well on both sides about 15 minutes. Remove chicken to platter, sprinkle with rye whiskey and let stand, turning to season evenly.

2. Pour off and discard all but 4 tablespoons fat from the pan. Cook sausages in casserole with onion until onion is wilted, stirring briskly. Add gizzards and hearts and cook, stirring for about 5 minutes. Add chicken livers and mushrooms and cook for 3 minutes.

3. Dissolve the bouillon in the boiling water and add to pan. Stir in rice and Parmesan cheese.

4. Push rice to sides of pan and return chicken to center of pan. Pour juices from platter over chicken, cover with rice, sprinkle with cheese. Simmer, partly covered with foil or lid, for 25 minutes. Yield: 4 servings.

1 (3½ pound) broiler-fryer chicken, cut-up or 3 pounds chicken breasts
1 teaspoon salt
½ teaspoon pepper
2 tablespoons butter
2 tablespoons olive oil
¼ cup rye whiskey
3 links sweet Italian sausage (discard casings), cut into 1 inch pieces
1 cup coarsely chopped onion
2 chicken gizzards, coarsely chopped
2 chicken hearts, coarsely chopped
2 chicken livers, coarsely chopped
1 cup sliced mushrooms
1 cup uncooked rice
3 tablespoons grated Parmesan cheese
3 chicken bouillon cubes
2½ cups boiling water

Chicken Enchiladas in Cream Sauce

2 tablespoons oil
2 onions, chopped
1 clove garlic, crushed
1 (4 ounce) can chopped
  green chiles
3 cups cooked, diced
  chicken
1 teaspoon sugar
1 (14½ ounce) can tomato
  sauce
  salt and pepper to taste
1 dozen corn tortillas
2 cups whipping cream
1½ cups half and half
5 chicken bouillon cubes
½ pound grated Monterey
  Jack cheese

1. Saute onions and garlic in skillet with 2 tablespoons oil. Add green chiles, chicken, sugar, tomato sauce, salt and pepper.

2. Soften tortillas by heating in a skillet with a small amount of bacon grease or oil. Remove and drain on a paper towel. Place chicken filling in corn tortilla, fold ends over and place seam side down in a 9x13 inch casserole. (Recipe may be made to this point early in the day. Chicken mixture may be made ahead and frozen.)

3. Heat whipping cream, half and half and bouillon cubes until bubbly and cubes are dissolved. Pour over tortillas and top with grated cheese. Bake at 350° for 35 to 40 minutes. Yield: 6 to 8 servings.

Broiled Deviled Chicken

½ cup Dijon mustard
1 cup oil
¼ cup honey
1 lemon, juice only
1 teaspoon freshly ground
  black pepper
2 tablespoons capers,
  finely chopped
6-8 garlic cloves, finely
  chopped
1 (2½-3 pound) chicken,
  cut into serving pieces
½ cup dried bread crumbs

1. Preheat broiler. Combine mustard, ½ cup of the oil, honey, lemon juice, pepper, capers and garlic. Mix well. Brush chicken generously with sauce. Arrange chicken pieces on rack over a shallow roasting pan. Broil for 7 minutes on each side, 3 to 4 inches from heat. Be careful not to burn.

2. Brush the chicken with the remaining oil and press bread crumbs on the chicken. Place chicken 4 to 6 inches from the broiler and broil for 8 to 10 minutes longer, carefully turning once or twice and watching that the crumbs do not burn. Test for doneness. Yield: 4 servings.

Optional: Just before serving, if desired, brush with melted butter or accompany with a mustard-flavored hollandaise sauce.

California Chicken and Fruit Cookout

1. Skin chicken if desired, grill over medium-high heat until almost done, basting with teriyaki sauce.

2. Prepare fruit. Halve and skin pears and peaches, skin and core pineapple and slice lengthwise. Slice papaya, mango and bananas.

3. Place each cooked chicken half on a large piece of foil. Divide fruit and place on top of chicken. Seal foil tightly to hold juices. Place in oven for 20 minutes at 350° so fruit cooks lightly and becomes juice or place on the barbecue grill and turn often to cook fruit.

4. Place a foil package on each guest's plate to be opened and savored for aroma and flavor. Serve with rice. Yield: 4 servings.

Note: Canned fruit can be substituted.

2 small chickens, halved
1 cup teriyaki sauce
2 fresh peaches
1 fresh pineapple
2 fresh pears
1 fresh papaya
1 fresh mango
2 fresh bananas (optional)
heavy duty aluminum foil

Chicken-Artichoke Casserole

1. Salt, pepper and paprika chicken pieces. Brown chicken in frying pan in 4 tablespoons of the butter. Place in large 4 quart casserole.

2. Heat remaining 2 tablespoons butter in frying pan and saute mushrooms for 5 minutes. Sprinkle flour over them and stir in chicken broth and sherry. Cook for 5 minutes.

3. Arrange artichoke hearts between chicken pieces. Pour mushroom-sherry sauce over them, cover and bake at 375° for 40 to 45 minutes. Yield: 4 to 6 servings.

3 pounds chicken fryer, cut up
1½ teaspoons salt
½ teaspoon paprika
¼ teaspoon pepper
6 tablespoons butter
¼ pound fresh mushrooms, sliced
2 tablespoons flour
⅔ cup chicken broth
3 tablespoons sherry
1 (14 ounce) can artichoke hearts, drained (not marinated)

Chicken Breast Ole

3 **large chicken breasts**
1 **(4 ounce) can diced green chiles, drained**
1 **(2½ ounce) can chopped black olives, drained**
¾ **cup Cheddar cheese, grated**
¾ **cup Monterey Jack cheese, grated**
3 **tablespoons chopped onion**
2-4 **tablespoons chopped cilantro**
⅓ **cup butter, melted**
¼ **teaspoon chili powder**
¼ **teaspoon cumin**
1 **cup tortilla chips, crumbled**
sour cream
taco sauce
chopped cilantro
lemon or lime wedges

1. Halve chicken breasts, remove bone and flatten. Preheat oven to 375°.

2. Combine chiles, olives and cheeses. Divide mixture among the 6 pieces of chicken, placing mixture down the center of each breast. Roll chicken around filling, folding in ends and securing with toothpicks.

3. Combine butter with chili powder and cumin. Coat chicken with butter mixture and roll in tortilla chips. Arrange chicken, seam-side down, in shallow greased casserole. Bake at 375° for 35 minutes, or until done.

4. Garnish with fresh chopped cilantro and lemon or lime wedges. Serve with sour cream and taco sauce in separate serving bowls. Yield: 4 to 6 servings.

Coq au Vin in Yogurt

4-6 **chicken breasts, skinned**
½ **cup dry white wine**
1½ **cups non fat yogurt**
½ **cup Dijon mustard**
1 **tablespoon fresh tarragon, thyme or oregano or a combination of the three herbs**

1. Place chicken in baking dish with wine. Combine yogurt with mustard and blend in herbs. Spoon over chicken breasts and bake in 350° oven for 50 minutes. Yield: 4 to 6 servings.

◊ Nutritional information per serving:

Calories 238	Fat .... 6 g	Iron .... 1 mg
Protein .... 36 g	Cholesterol .... 90 mg	Potassium .... 367 mg
Carbohydrates .... 5 g	Calcium .... 131 mg	Sodium .... 245 mg

Bleu Cheese Chicken

1. Cream together the bleu cheese, 5 tablespoons of the butter and cream cheese using steel blade of food processor. Add nutmeg and blend. Form into 6 oval pieces and roll in Swiss cheese. Put on waxed paper and chill 1½ hours.

2. Flatten the chicken breasts between waxed paper and spread each breast lightly with Dijon mustard. In the center of each breast, place a chilled cheese oval and enclose it with the chicken breast, secure with toothpicks.

3. Roll each chicken breast in the flour, then the egg, then the bread crumbs and place on a plate. Chill for at least 1 hour.

4. In a frying pan, sear the chilled breast in 4 tablespoons of the butter for 2 to 3 minutes, or until they are lightly browned. Transfer to an oblong baking dish and bake at 400° for 10 to 12 minutes. Do not overcook or the cheese will run out. Yield: 4 to 6 servings.

- **5 ounces bleu cheese (room temperature)**
- **9 tablespoons butter**
- **¾ cup cream cheese dash of nutmeg**
- **¾ cup grated Swiss cheese**
- **3 chicken breasts, split, skinned and boned**
- **2-3 tablespoons Dijon mustard**
- **1 egg, lightly beaten**
- **⅓ cup flour**
- **¼ cup unseasoned bread crumbs**

Chicken Breasts Stuffed with Mushroom Duxelles

½ **pound mushrooms**
½ **cup butter, melted**
⅛ **teaspoon salt**
⅛ **teaspoon pepper**
⅛ **teaspoon dry mustard**
4 **chicken breasts, split, skinned and boned**
¾ **cup round butter-flavored crackers, crushed into crumbs**
⅓ **cup grated Parmesan cheese**

1. Mince mushrooms in food processor using steel blade. Cook in 2 tablespoons butter until liquid has evaporated, add salt, pepper and mustard. Let cool.

2. Find the small piece (filet) of breast meat that is attached to the main part of the breast meat and forms a pocket. Place a spoonful of the mushroom mixture in the pocket. Press the two pieces together.

3. Mix the cracker crumbs with the cheese, brush the chicken with the remaining butter and roll in the crumb mixture.

4. Place in a baking dish and bake at 400° for 20 to 25 minutes. Yield: 4 servings.

Chicken Florentine

¾ **cup Italian seasoned breadcrumbs**
¼ **cup grated Parmesan cheese**
6 **whole chicken breasts, boned, skinned, split**
½ **cup sliced green onion**
2 **tablespoons butter**
2 **tablespoons flour**
2 **cups milk**
1 **(10 ounce) package frozen chopped spinach, thawed and drained**
4 **ounces ham, diced**

1. Combine bread crumbs and cheese. Dip chicken breasts in crumb mixture to coat slightly. Arrange in 9x13 inch baking pan, reserving remaining crumb mixture.

2. In a saucepan, cook onions in butter until softened. Blend in flour, stir in milk all at once, cook and stir until thickened and bubbly. Cook and stir one minute longer. Stir in spinach and ham. Spoon mixture over chicken, sprinkle with remaining crumbs.

3. Bake at 350° for 40 to 45 minutes or until done. Yield: 8 to 10 servings.

Oriental Chicken

1. Season chicken with garlic salt, paprika and pepper. Saute in vegetable oil until brown and tender. Add onion, mushrooms, green pepper, celery and ½ cup of the broth. Cover and steam for 1½ minutes.

2. Blend remaining broth with cornstarch and soy sauce. Stir into chicken-vegetable mixture. Cook and stir about 1 minute until thickened. Add tomatoes and heat through.

3. Serve immediately over steamed rice, garnish with chopped parsley. Yield: 4 to 6 servings.

1½ pounds chicken breast meat, boned and cut into bite-sized pieces
1 teaspoon garlic salt
1 teaspoon paprika
¼ teaspoon pepper
2 tablespoons vegetable oil
1 medium onion, sliced
¼ pound mushrooms, sliced
1 large green pepper, diced
1 cup sliced celery
1 cup chicken broth
2 tablespoons cornstarch
3 tablespoons soy sauce
2 large tomatoes, cut into wedges
chopped parsley
steamed rice

◊ Nutritional information per serving:

Calories 280	Fat .... 10 g	Iron .... 2 mg
Protein .... 35 g	Cholesterol .... 87 mg	Potassium .... 542 mg
Carbohydrates .... 9 g	Calcium .... 37 mg	Sodium .... 1096 mg

Papaya Chicken

½ **teaspoon paprika**
½ **teaspoon ground ginger**
1 **teaspoon salt**
3 **whole chicken breasts, halved, skinned, boned and cut into thirds**
1 **large or 2 small papayas**
1½ **tablespoons lime or lemon juice**
½ **cup chutney**
1½ **cups chicken broth**
1 **teaspoon cornstarch**
2 **tablespoons butter**
2 **tablespoons vegetable oil**
cooked rice
½ **cup sliced almonds, toasted**

1. Mix paprika, ginger and salt; sprinkle over chicken.

2. Peel and seed papaya, cut lengthwise into eight pieces, then cut each piece crosswise. Put fruit into bowl and add lime or lemon juice and mix until well-coated. Finely chop chutney and combine in small bowl with broth and cornstarch. This can be done ahead and refrigerated separately.

3. Heat frying pan to 325° on medium-low heat. Add butter and oil and heat until bubbly. Add chicken and cook until lightly browned, 3 to 4 minutes on each side. Then cook another 4 to 5 minutes until cooked through.

4. Uncover, and stir in chutney mixture, bring to a boil, stirring until thickened. Add fruit and cook, stirring gently until fruit is glazed and heated through. Serve over rice and top each serving with almonds. Yield: 6 to 8 servings.

Classic Chicken Breasts

1. Season chicken breasts with salt and pepper, then dredge in flour. Save remaining flour.

2. In a medium skillet, brown chicken in 3 tablespoons butter, remove and add onion and saute briefly. Add wine.

3. Over high heat, cook liquid until almost evaporated. Deglaze pan, scraping loose browned bits of meat. Add remainder of flour and stir until thickened. Add tarragon and chicken broth. Stir until smooth.

4. Return chicken to skillet, cover and simmer 20 minutes, or until tender. Remove chicken and keep warm. Add last tablespoon of butter, cream and heat, stirring. Pour sauce over chicken. Yield: 4 servings.

2 **whole chicken breasts, halved, boned and skinned**
salt and fresh ground pepper to taste
¼ **cup flour**
4 **tablespoons butter**
1 **tablespoon minced onion**
¼ **cup dry white wine**
1 **teaspoon dried tarragon**
¼ **cup chicken broth**
¼ **cup heavy cream**

Parmesan Chicken Strips

1. Stir garlic into sour cream and allow to marinate 1 hour or longer.

2. Add Worcestershire sauce, celery salt, and paprika into sour cream mixture.

3. Mix breadcrumbs with Parmesan cheese. Dip chicken in sour cream mixture, then roll in breadcrumbs.

4. Melt butter in baking dish, arrange chicken in dish and bake at 350° for 35 minutes. Yield: 4 servings.

2 **cloves garlic, minced**
½ **cup sour cream**
1 **tablespoon Worcester-shire sauce**
1 **tablespoon celery salt**
1 **tablespoon paprika**
½ **cup Parmesan cheese**
1 **cup fine breadcrumbs**
½ **cup butter**
5 **boneless chicken breasts, cut in strips**

Baked Chicken with Cheese and Mushrooms

½ **pound fresh mush-
   rooms, sliced**
6 **tablespoons butter**
4 **whole chicken breasts,
   skinned, boned and
   halved**
½ **cup grated Parmesan
   cheese**
2 **eggs, beaten**
1 **cup Italian-seasoned
   bread crumbs**
½ **pound Swiss cheese
   (Monterey Jack may be
   substituted), sliced**
½ **cup sherry**

1. Saute mushrooms in 2 tablespoons of the butter and set aside.

2. Coat chicken in Parmesan cheese, then dip in eggs, then in bread crumbs. Brown in butter, then place in baking dish.

3. Cover with sliced Swiss cheese, then sauteed mushrooms. Bake at 350° for 15 minutes. Add sherry and bake 15 minutes longer. Yield: 6 to 8 servings.

Spicy Mustard Chicken

3 **whole chicken breasts,
   halved**
½ **cup honey**
½ **cup Dijon mustard**
1 **tablespoon curry pow-
   der**
2-4 **tablespoons soy sauce**

1. Place chicken skin side down in 9x13 inch baking dish, in one layer.

2. Mix marinade by combining honey, mustard, curry powder and soy sauce. Pour over chicken and refrigerate overnight.

3. Before baking, turn chicken breasts over, cover dish with foil and bake at 350° for 30 minutes. Uncover, baste and continue baking for 15 minutes or until done. Yield: 4 to 6 servings.

◊ Nutritional information per serving:

Calories 436	Fat .... 10 g	Iron .... 3 mg
Protein .... 60 g	Cholesterol .... 159 mg	Potassium .... 539 mg
Carbohydrates .... 26 g	Calcium .... 54 mg	Sodium .... 923 mg

California Gold Chicken with Avocado Sauce

1. In frying pan, combine water, wine, curry powder, salt, peppercorns and parsley. Bring to a boil, reduce heat to medium-high. Add chicken and poach for 5 minutes on each side. Remove, drain. Chill.

2. Peel and seed avocados. Cut into chunks and put in food processor with steel blade or in a blender. Add mayonnaise, sour cream, sherry, lemon juice and parsley. Puree until smooth. Add salt and pepper to taste.

3. Serve on bed of red lettuce with sauce poured over top. Yield: 6 servings.

½ cup plus 2 tablespoons water
1¼ cups dry white wine
1¼ teaspoons curry powder
½ teaspoon salt
8 whole black peppercorns
4 sprigs parsley
6 whole chicken breasts, boned, skinned and halved
2 ripe avocados
2 tablespoons mayonnaise
1 cup sour cream
1 tablespoon dry sherry
2 tablespoons lemon juice
2 tablespoons chopped parsley
ground white pepper and salt to taste
red lettuce

Country Chicken

1. Roll chicken breasts in flour mixture. Fry in hot shortening until browned. Drain on paper towels.

2. In same pan, saute onions, green peppers and garlic until transparent. Stir in salt, pepper and thyme, mix well. Add tomatoes and fresh parsley.

3. Place breasts in 9x13 inch baking dish and cover with sauce. Cover and bake at 350° for 45 minutes. Serve with rice. Yield: 8 servings.

6 chicken breasts, halved, boned and skinned
2 cups flour, seasoned with salt and pepper
½ cup vegetable shortening
2 onions, finely chopped
2 green peppers, finely chopped
3 cloves garlic, minced
3 teaspoons salt
½ teaspoon white pepper
½ teaspoon thyme
2 (1 pound 13 ounce) cans stewed tomatoes
1 tablespoon finely chopped parsley

Roast Chicken with Potatoes and Rosemary

1 **chicken, cut up, or substitute chicken thighs**
6 **large red potatoes, cut into wedges**
1-2 **yellow onions, cut into wedges**
1-2 **cloves garlic, cut in half**
4 **carrots, quartered lengthwise, and halved**
1 **red pepper, cored, seeded and cut into strips**
seasoned salt and pepper to taste
olive oil (as needed, up to ⅓ cup)
fresh rosemary
fresh lime slices

1. Place chicken, potatoes, onions, garlic, carrots and red pepper in a large, greased baking dish. Season well with salt and pepper, then drizzle with olive oil. Place fresh rosemary sprigs on top and roast at 425° until well browned and tender, turning and basting as needed, approximately 40 to 45 minutes.

2. Serve with fresh lime slices and fresh bread to soak up the juices. Yield: 4 servings.

Orange-Dijon Delight

1 **chicken, cut into serving pieces, skinned**
1 **(12 ounce) can frozen orange juice concentrate, thawed**
1-2 **tablespoons Dijon mustard**
2-4 **tablespoons fresh tarragon or 1-2 teaspoons dried**

1. Combine orange juice, mustard and tarragon, add chicken and marinate for 30 minutes to overnight.

2. Place chicken parts in a single layer in a broiler pan or on a barbecue grill. Broil or barbecue until done. Yield: 4 servings.

◊ Nutritional information per serving:

Calories 415	Fat .... 8 g	Iron .... 2 mg
Protein .... 52 g	Cholesterol .... 130 mg	Potassium .... 914 mg
Carbohydrates .... 33 g	Calcium .... 65 mg	Sodium .... 211 mg

Orange-Glazed Cornish Hens with Pecan-Cornbread Stuffing

1. Heat apple juice in saucepan, and add brandy and butter. When butter is melted, add to the stuffing mix. Add pecans and mix well. Stuff Cornish hens and roast for 1 to 1½ hours at 350°.

2. Meanwhile, prepare orange sauce. Combine sugars in saucepan, and add cornstarch, orange rind, juice, liqueur and salt. Simmer until transparent and slightly thickened.

3. Baste hens in oven with sauce for last 10 minutes of baking. Serve with additional sauce at table. Yield: 6 servings.

1 **cup apple juice**
¼ **cup apricot brandy**
¼ **cup butter**
1 **(8 ounce) package cornbread stuffing mix**
¾ **cup pecans, chopped**
6 **Cornish hens**

Orange Sauce:
¼ **cup brown sugar**
¼ **cup white sugar**
2 **tablespoons cornstarch**
2 **tablespoons grated orange rind**
1½ **cups orange juice**
½ **cup Cointreau, Grand Marnier or Triple Sec**
½ **teaspoon salt**

Cranberry Chutney
(serve with pork or poultry)

1. Combine sugar, water, cranberries, pineapple chunks, lemon rind, and spices in a 3 quart saucepan. Cook over moderate heat until berries begin to pop and mixture starts to thicken, approximately 20 minutes. Add onion slices and pecan halves, and simmer 20 minutes longer, or until chutney is as thick as desired.

2. Cover, cool and refrigerate, or ladle into sterilized jelly glasses and seal immediately with melted paraffin.

3. Serve with chicken, turkey, or pork. Yield: 12 to 14 servings.

1⅔ **cups sugar**
1 **cup water**
4 **cups fresh cranberries**
1 **cup pineapple chunks**
1 **teaspoon grated lemon rind**
1 **teaspoon ground ginger**
½ **teaspoon allspice**
1 **stick cinnamon**
1 **onion, thinly sliced**
½ **cup pecan halves**

Grilled Turkey Tenderloins

**4 turkey tenderloins
(about 1¼ to 1½ pounds)
4 tablespoons margarine
2 large cloves garlic,
crushed
salt and pepper
4 sliced shallots
½ pound mushrooms,
sliced
¼ cup chopped parsley**

1. Rinse tenderloins and pat dry. Melt 2 tablespoons of the butter with garlic and brush on meat. Season with salt and pepper. Grill over hot coals, turning occasionally and basting with butter until golden brown.

2. While meat is cooking, melt 2 tablespoons butter in skillet. Add shallots and cook until soft. Add mushrooms and cook 2 to 3 minutes. Turn up heat and cook until liquid has evaporated.

3. Remove tenderloins from grill and top with mushrooms and parsley. Yield: 4 servings.

Alternative: Omit shallot-mushroom sauce and serve on French rolls for elegant turkey sandwiches. Use Basil Mayonnaise (see Salads and Dressings).

◊ Nutritional information per serving:

Calories 336	Fat ....24 g	Iron ....3 mg
Protein ....33 g	Cholesterol ....93 mg	Potassium ....747 mg
Carbohydrates ....10 g	Calcium ....74 mg	Sodium ....1093 mg

Turkey Cutlets

1. Combine cheese, egg, 1 table-spoon oil, parsley, salt and pepper. Blend well.

2. Pound cutlets to ⅛ inch thick, dip in flour, then beaten egg, then bread crumbs.

3. Melt butter and oil in frying pan and cook cutlets 2 to 3 minutes per side over medium-high heat. Add more oil if needed.

4. Remove cutlets to warm platter. Pour lemon juice into pan juices and stir to deglaze pan. Pour pan juices over cutlets, garnish with parsley and serve. Yield: 4 servings.

4-6 tablespoons grated Parmesan cheese
1 beaten egg
1 tablespoon vegetable oil
¾ cup bread crumbs
2 teaspoons minced parsley
1 teaspoon salt
¼ teaspoon pepper
1 pound turkey breast, cut into cutlets
¼ cup flour
¼ cup butter
2-3 tablespoons olive oil
1 lemon, juice only fresh parsley

Note: It is easier to cut turkey into cutlets if partially frozen.

Barbecue Sauce

1. Combine ingredients in a jar with a tight fitting lid. Keep mixed when using. May be used as a marinade and as a basting sauce for chicken, fish, ribs, etc.

2. Recipe may be made in larger quantity and stored on shelf for at least a month. Yield: 1¾ cups.

1 cup vinegar
¼ cup vegetable oil
2 tablespoons salt
2 tablespoons sugar
1 tablespoon brown sugar
1 tablespoon chili powder
1 teaspoon black pepper
½ teaspoon white pepper
¼ teaspoon oregano
¼ teaspoon paprika

Onion-Raisin Conserve
(to serve with pork or poultry)

½ cup raisins
¼ cup brandy
½ cup fresh tangerine or
    orange juice
4 tablespoons unsalted
    butter
1 red onion, thinly sliced
    lengthwise
1 bulb fennel, halved,
    cored, and thinly sliced
    lengthwise
1 teaspoon sugar
    salt and freshly ground
    black pepper

1. Soak raisins in brandy for 20 minutes to plump them.

2. Melt butter in skillet and saute onion for 5 minutes (not until soft). Add fennel and saute over medium heat for 5 minutes more.

3. Add raisins and juice. Stir in sugar. Add salt and pepper to taste.

4. Serve warm. Yield: 6 servings.

Onion Jam
(to serve with pork or poultry)

¼   cup butter
2   tablespoons olive oil
8   large red onions, thinly
     sliced
2-3 sprigs fresh rosemary
     (optional)
2   teaspoons salt
½   teaspoon freshly ground
     pepper
2   tablespoons packed
     brown sugar

1. Heat butter and oil in large skillet, add onions. Saute until they begin to brown, reduce heat. Stir in salt and pepper.

2. Cook, partially covered, stirring frequently, until onions turn caramel color and are very soft, about 30 minutes. Stir in brown sugar until dissolved. Yield: 6 cups.

Optional: Add 2 to 3 sprigs fresh rosemary to onions while cooking. Remove when done.

Meats

MEAT

This is the favorite category of those dwelling in the oldest wine regions of the world because it gives them an opportunity and excuse to sample their well-aged reds with fine cuisine. Few taste experiences can compare with the marriage of a great, mature Cabernet Sauvignon with Stuffed Filet of Beef, or Pinot Noir with a lighter style Veal Marsala, or Merlot with meat in a subtle red wine sauce. A few other ideas:

Barbecue — Petite Sirah for the spiciest ingredients; beer if it goes beyond that.

Hamburger — Quaffing wines; plus Zinfandel, Gamay, Barbera.

Lamb chops — Mid-range reds, including Zinfandel, Barbera.

Lamb, rack — Big wines, such as a great Cabernet Sauvignon.

Liver — A fat Merlot or softer, older Zinfandel; a mid-bodied Pinot Noir; a lighter Cabernet Sauvignon.

Pork chops — Depending on the sauce, choose from the light and fruity side of the spectrum (Johannisberg Riesling; Gamay).

Pork loin — A delicate, aged Pinot Noir.

Prime rib — A mid-range Cabernet or Pinot Noir.

Steak — Depending upon the quality of the cut and the style of preparation, you can range from a good Zinfandel, to an aged Pinot Noir, to the Merlot and Cabernet Sauvignon.

Veal — Johannisberg Riesling can complement the lightest dishes, followed by a lighter Sauvignon Blanc; red sauces need to be balanced by a good Zinfandel, Merlot or Cabernet.

Steak with Green Peppercorn Sauce

1. Heat a heavy skillet on medium-high heat. Sprinkle lightly with salt. Add steaks. Cook 2 minutes, turn. Cook 4 to 7 minutes to desired doneness. Remove to platter, keep warm.

2. Add butter to same skillet. When melted, add onions or shallots. Add mustard, peppercorns, wine, and whipping cream, stir. Cook over medium heat until reduced and thickened.

3. Place steaks on heated serving plate. Stir juice from meat into sauce, spoon sauce over steaks and serve immediately.

4 (6-8 ounce) sirloin steaks, 1 inch thick
  salt to taste
3 tablespoons butter
2-3 tablespoons chopped shallots or green onions
2-3 heaping tablespoons Dijon mustard
1-3 tablespoons canned green peppercorns, drained
¼ cup white wine
1 cup whipping cream

California Barbecued Brisket

1. Place beef in roaster or Dutch oven, cover with water. Add rosemary and bay leaves. Add garlic and bring to a boil, reduce heat and simmer, covered, about 2½ hours or until meat is tender. Drain, pat dry. (May be prepared ahead of time and refrigerated.)

2. Cook onion and green pepper in hot oil in small saucepan until softened. Stir in tomato sauce, plum or grape jelly, vinegar, chili powder and Worcestershire sauce. Bring to boil, reduce by half.

3. In a covered grill, arrange preheated coals around drip pan, test for slow heat above pan. Place brisket on grill over pan, but not over coals, cover, cook 20 to 25 minutes, turning and brushing occasionally with the sauce. Yield: 6 to 8 servings.

1 (4-5 pound) beef brisket
2 teaspoons crushed dried rosemary
2 bay leaves
4 cloves garlic, minced
1 cup chopped onion
1 cup chopped green pepper
2 tablespoons vegetable oil
1 cup tomato sauce
1 cup plum or grape jelly
4 tablespoons vinegar
2 tablespoons chili powder
2 teaspoons Worcestershire sauce

Beef Brisket in Beer

5 pounds beef brisket
2 teaspoons salt
¼ teaspoon pepper
2 onions, sliced
4 ribs celery, chopped
1 cup chili sauce
1 (12 ounce) can beer
2 tablespoons brown
  sugar
2 cloves garlic, crushed

1. Place beef in roaster, fat side up. Season with salt and pepper, and top with sliced onions and celery.

2. Combine chili sauce, beer, brown sugar and garlic and pour over meat. Cover and bake at 325° for 3½ hours, basting often. Uncover and bake another 30 to 45 minutes. Yield: 6 to 8 servings.

Note: Can be made a day ahead, degreased and reheated. Makes great sandwiches, served with horseradish. Also, good sliced and served in flour tortillas with sour cream and tomatoes.

Enchilada Pie

1 pound ground beef
1 onion, chopped
1 clove garlic, chopped
2 teaspoons salt
¼ teaspoon pepper
1 tablespoon chili powder
2½ cups Monterey Jack or
  Cheddar cheese (add 3
  cups if you wish)
1 (8 ounce) can tomato
  sauce
1 (4 ounce) can chopped
  black olives
6 tortillas (spread with
  butter)
1 cup beef broth

1. Brown beef, onion and garlic in frying pan, drain grease. Add seasonings and tomato sauce.

2. In medium casserole, alternate layers of tortillas, meat sauce, olives and cheese. Add broth, cover and bake for 20 minutes at 400°. Yield: 4 to 6 servings.

Picante Chili

1. Brown the onion in oil or butter in large skillet until soft. Transfer to crockpot. Brown cubed steak and ground beef, a little at a time, in the same skillet. Transfer to crockpot.

2. Combine the remaining ingredients and simmer until the chocolate melts. Add to crockpot and mix well. Cook for 7 to 10 hours on low setting. Yield: 6 to 8 servings.

1 **large onion, chopped**
2 **tablespoons oil or butter**
1 **pound steak, cut into ½ inch cubes**
1 **pound ground beef**
1 **(8 ounce) can tomato sauce**
1 **(28 ounce) can tomatoes**
1 **tablespoon chili powder**
2 **tablespoons cilantro or parsley, chopped**
1 **cup hot picante sauce, or to taste**
1 **clove garlic, minced**
½ **teaspoon salt**
½ **teaspoon oregano**
1 **ounce Mexican chocolate, grated (or substitute baking chocolate with 1 teaspoon sugar and ½ teaspoon cinnamon)**
1 **cup grated Cheddar or Monterey Jack cheese — up to ½ cup more may be used (optional)**

Note: Transports well in the crockpot and will stay hot for several hours. Serve with cornbread and a green or fruit salad.

Stuffed Filet of Beef

3 tablespoons butter
3 tablespoons vegetable oil
2 onions, finely chopped
¼ pound ham, finely chopped
1 (2 ounce) tin anchovies, drained and coarsely chopped
1 (4 ounce) can black olives
1 large clove garlic, minced
1 teaspoon thyme
½ teaspoon rosemary
¼ cup fresh parsley, chopped
2 eggs, lightly beaten
1 (5-6 pound) beef tender-loin

1. In a heavy skillet, heat butter and oil and saute onion until limp. Add the ham, anchovies, garlic, olives, thyme and rosemary and cook for 4 minutes. Add the parsley and remove from heat. Stir in the eggs and continue cooking and stirring until the mixture is thickened.

2. Slice the tenderloin part way through, into 8 or 9 slices. Leave about 1 inch uncut at bottom. Stuff each incision with the mixture and tie with string. Place on rack or broiling pan and roast at 350° for 45 minutes.

3. Remove string and slice through. Garnish with watercress or parsley. Yield: 6 to 8 servings.

Stir-Fried Beef and Pea Pods

1. Slice flank steak into thin strips 2 to 2½ inches wide by ⅛ inch thick, cutting across the grain. Steak is easier to slice if it is partially frozen.

2. Blend together ingredients for marinade and mix with meat. Marinate beef slices for at least 1 hour or up to 2 days.

3. In measuring cup or small bowl, mix together the ingredients for the gravy.

4. Heat wok or large frying pan, add oil. Add marinated beef and stir-fry for 1 minute or until meat has just started turning brown. Add pea pods and stir-fry for 30 seconds (1 minute if using broccoli). Add chicken broth and continue stirring until broth boils. Cover and cook for 1 minute (3 minutes if using broccoli).

5. Add gravy, turn off heat. Stir until gravy thickens, about 15 to 20 seconds. Serve immediately, with rice. Yield: 4 servings.

1 pound flank steak
2 tablespoons vegetable or peanut oil
20 snow peas (pea pods) or 1 pound broccoli, cut into 1½ inch pieces
⅓ cup chicken broth

Marinade:
1 tablespoon cornstarch
1 teaspoon sugar
¼ teaspoon salt
¼ teaspoon sesame oil
2 tablespoons white wine or sherry
1 tablespoon soy sauce
1 tablespoon oyster sauce
⅛ teaspoon white pepper
¼ teaspoon garlic powder
1-2 tablespoons water

Gravy:
3 teaspoons cornstarch
1 teaspoon soy sauce
¼ teaspoon salt
¼-½cup water

◊ Nutritional information per serving:

Calories 319	Fat .... 16 g	Iron .... 4 mg
Protein .... 34 g	Cholesterol .... 94 mg	Potassium ....541 mg
Carbohydrates ....6 g	Calcium .... 18 mg	Sodium .... 490 mg

Oriental Stir-Fry with Noodles

1 **(16 ounce) package Chinese noodles**
4 **tablespoons peanut oil**
½ **pound boneless pork, thinly sliced (chicken or beef may be substituted)**
1 **green pepper, thinly sliced**
2 **stalks celery, diagonally sliced**
1 **onion, thinly sliced**
6 **mushrooms, sliced**
1 **(6 ounce) can sliced bamboo shoots**
1 **(6 ounce) can sliced water chestnuts**
½ **pound bean sprouts**
¾ **cup water**
1 **teaspoon chicken bouillon granules**
2 **tablespoons cornstarch**
2 **tablespoons soy sauce**
1 **teaspoon MSG (optional)**
½ **teaspoon salt**
⅛ **teaspoon pepper**

1. Cook noodles according to package directions. Drain, rinse in cold water, set aside.

2. Over high heat, heat 2 tablespoons of the oil in a wok or large skillet. Add meat, green pepper, celery and onion. Fry about 5 minutes, stirring constantly. Add mushrooms, bamboo shoots, water chestnuts and bean sprouts. Continue frying about 2 minutes, stirring constantly. Add ½ cup of the water and chicken bouillon, cook and stir for 3 minutes longer.

3. Dissolve the cornstarch in ¼ cup of the water, add to vegetable mixture along with the soy sauce, MSG, salt and pepper. Continue cooking and stirring until thick, about 1 minute. Turn heat to very low.

4. In a separate skillet, heat the remaining 2 tablespoons of oil. Over high heat, fry noodles until lightly golden. Add noodles to vegetables, toss gently. Serve immediately. Yield: 6 servings.

◊ Nutritional information per serving:

Calories 597	Fat ....32 g	Iron ....2 mg
Protein ....25 g	Cholesterol ....46 mg	Potassium ....51 mg
Carbohydrates ....57 g	Calcium ....49 mg	Sodium ....1394 mg

Sausage, Pepper, Olive Saute

1. Cut sausage into 1 inch pieces. Brown in large skillet until cooked through. Remove from pan and set aside.

2. Pour all fat from skillet, add 2 tablespoons olive oil. Heat oil and add onions, pepper and garlic to pan. Cook over medium-high heat for 1 to 2 minutes. Add olives and mushrooms and cook 1 to 2 minutes longer.

3. Return sausage to pan, add wine. Cover, cook over high heat to reduce liquid by about half. Remove pan from heat, stir in basil or parsley.

4. Serve immediately over linguine, thin spaghetti or rice with plenty of French bread to soak up the sauce. Yield: 4 servings.

1½ pounds mild or hot Italian sausage
2 tablespoons olive oil
1 medium onion, thinly sliced into rings
1 large red bell pepper, cut into thin strips
2 cloves garlic, minced
¾ cup ripe olives, cut in half
¼ cup Madeira or dry vermouth
2 tablespoons chopped fresh basil or parsley
1 pound sliced fresh mushrooms (optional)
linguine, thin spaghetti or rice

Apricot Pork Roast

1. Season roast with salt and pepper and rub with mustard. Combine orange juice, soy sauce, garlic and ginger. Pour over roast and marinate overnight.

2. Preheat oven to 350°. Place roast in baking pan, pour marinade over top and bake 40 to 45 minutes per pound or until internal temperature reaches 160°.

3. Meanwhile, combine jam, orange juice, lemon juice and pan juices and boil for 5 minutes. Remove roast from oven and baste with jam mixture. Repeat basting for next half hour, every five minutes. Slice and serve. Yield: 4 to 6 servings.

1 (4-5 pound) boneless pork roast
salt and pepper to taste
2 tablespoons Dijon mustard
½ cup orange juice
¼ cup soy sauce
1 clove garlic, minced
2 tablespoons ground ginger

Basting Sauce:
1 (10 ounce) jar apricot jam
2 tablespoons orange juice
2 tablespoons lemon juice

Pork and Bean Threads with Hot Bean Sauce

2 ounces bean threads or rice sticks, cut into 4 inch lengths
6 dried mushrooms
½ pound pork loin, finely chopped
2-3 cloves garlic, minced
1 small dry hot red chile, seeded and chopped
2 tablespoons fresh minced ginger
3 tablespoons vegetable oil
1-2 teaspoons hot bean sauce
3 whole green onions, thinly sliced
½ cup chicken broth
1 tablespoon sherry or white wine
1 tablespoon soy sauce
2 teaspoons sesame oil

1. Soak bean threads or rice sticks in water for 30 minutes, drain. Soak mushrooms 1 hour, drain, squeeze dry and thinly slice.

2. Place the pork, garlic, red chile, ginger in a food processor and process until minced.

3. Heat wok or large flat frying pan, add 3 tablespoons oil. Add pork mixture and hot bean sauce and stir-fry until pork turns opaque. Stir in mushrooms, bean threads, green onions, chicken broth, sherry and soy sauce. Simmer 5 minutes or until all liquid is absorbed into noodles.

4. Stir in sesame oil just before serving. Yield: 4 to 6 servings.

Chile Verde

1. Coat pork cubes with flour. Brown in oil in a large heavy skillet, add seasonings, chiles, chopped onion and salsa. If necessary, add water, cover and simmer about 45 minutes, again adding water if necessary.

2. Serve over rice or in heated flour tortillas with condiments such as sour cream, cilantro, and black olives. Yield: 4 to 6 servings.

3 large pork chops, cut into ¼ inch strips
¼ cup flour
¼ cup oil
2 (7 ounce) cans chopped green chiles
1 medium yellow onion, chopped
1 (10 ounce) can red salsa
1-3 cloves garlic, minced
salt and pepper to taste
rice or flour tortillas
sour cream
cilantro
black olives

Note: Can also be served as hors d'oeuvres with sturdy tortilla chips.

◊ Nutritional information per serving:

Calories 472	Fat .... 36 g	Iron .... 2 mg
Protein .... 32 g	Cholesterol .... 110 mg	Potassium .... 553 mg
Carbohydrates .... 5 g	Calcium .... 22 mg	Sodium .... 461 mg

Pork Loin with Piquant Sauce

2 **pork loin roasts, boned and tied together (6 to 7 pounds total weight)**
3 **tablespoons flour**
1 **teaspoon sage**
1 **teaspoon dry mustard**
1 **teaspoon salt**
½ **teaspoon pepper**

Sauce:
1 **cup dry white wine**
1 **cup apple juice**
1 **cup soy sauce**
2 **teaspoons powdered ginger**
1 **teaspoon dried thyme**
6 **cloves garlic, minced pinch dry mustard**

1. In small bowl, combine flour, sage, dry mustard, salt and pepper. Rub roast with the mixed dry ingredients.

2. In saucepan, warm ingredients for sauce over medium heat.

3. Prepare barbecue for indirect grilling method. Place roast on rack and grill, basting with sauce, for about 1½ hours to 2 hours, or until thermometer reaches 160°.

4. Slice and serve with a little sauce spooned over meat. Pass remaining sauce separately. Yield: 10 to 12 servings.

Note: Meat can be prepared in oven. Bake at 325° for approximately 2½ hours or until 160° on thermometer. Leftover meat can be made into a great salad or sandwiches.

Luau Pork Ambrosia

1. Place roast in marinating dish. Combine 2 of the jars of apricot baby food, honey, lemon juice, soy sauce, garlic, onion, ginger ale, ginger and pepper. Pour over pork and marinate 4 to 5 hours, turning occasionally.

2. Line grill with foil, let coals burn down until covered with gray ashes.

3. Remove pork from marinade, reserve. Place roast on spit and cook over low coals for about 3½ hours or until the internal temperature reaches 185°. During last half hour, baste frequently with sauce. During last 5 minutes, spread one jar apricots over meat.

4. Mix reserved marinade with last jar apricots and heat, serve as sauce over meat.

5. While marinade is heating, heat whole apricots and lemon rind together. Garnish meat with whole apricots, sprinkle with coconut and parsley. Yield: 8 to 10 servings.

1 **(5 pound) pork roast**
4 **(4½ ounce) jars strained apricots, baby food**
⅓ **cup honey**
¼ **cup fresh lemon juice**
¼ **cup soy sauce**
½ **clove garlic, minced**
1 **small onion, minced**
⅛ **teaspoon ginger**
1 **cup ginger ale**
⅛ **teaspoon pepper**
1 **(1 pound 13 ounce) can whole apricots**
1 **tablespoon grated lemon rind**
¼ **cup grated coconut parsley sprigs**

Crown Roast of Pork

1 (16 rib) Crown Roast of pork (ask butcher to prepare the crown form)

Apple and Onion Stuffing:
- **1 cup raisins**
- **¾ cup butter, melted**
- **1 cup chopped onion**
- **1 clove garlic, minced**
- **1 cup celery, chopped**
- **7 cups soft bread crumbs (9 slices of bread)**
- **3 cups diced tart apples**
- **¼ cup chopped parsley**
- **½ teaspoon salt**
- **¼ teaspoon paprika parsley or watercress (for garnish) crabapples (for garnish)**

1. Preheat oven to 450°. Wrap a piece of foil around ends of each bone to keep them from burning. Put roast in oven and reduce heat to 350°, allowing cooking time of 30 minutes per pound or approximately 3 hours.

2. Soak raisins in boiling water for 5 minutes, then drain. Melt butter and saute onions, garlic, and celery for 3 minutes. Toss with raisins and bread, apples, parsley, salt and paprika. The stuffing can be made one day ahead.

3. One hour before roast is done, remove from oven and fill cavity with apple and onion stuffing. Return roast to oven and continue cooking for one hour. Transfer meat to serving platter and garnish with parsley or watercress and crabapples. Yield: 10 to 16 servings.

Mustard-Rosemary Barbecued Leg of Lamb

1 whole leg of lamb, boned and butterflied by butcher (about 6 pounds)

Marinade:
- **4 tablespoons Dijon mustard**
- **4 tablespoons tarragon vinegar**
- **4 tablespoons olive oil**
- **1 clove garlic, minced**
- **3 sprigs fresh rosemary, chopped seasoned salt and pepper mint jelly (optional)**

1. Mix together marinade ingredients and marinate lamb overnight in refrigerator or several hours at room temperature. Turn often. Bring to room temperature before grilling.

2. Grill over medium heat for 20 minutes on each side, or until medium-rare, basting often with marinade. Let stand 10 minutes before carving across the grain into very thin slices.

3. Serve with mint jelly. Yield: 6 to 8 servings.

Barbecued Leg of Lamb with Currant Jelly Sauce

1. Mix together marinade ingredients and marinate lamb overnight in refrigerator or several hours at room temperature. Turn often.

2. Grill over medium heat for 20 minutes on each side, or until medium-rare, basting often with marinade.

3. Meanwhile, combine the ingredients for the sauce in a small saucepan and heat.

4. When roast is done, remove from heat and let stand for 10 minutes before carving. Serve with sauce. Yield: 6 to 8 servings.

1 whole leg of lamb, boned and butterflied by butcher (about 6 pounds)

Marinade:
1 cup dry red wine
½ cup olive oil
2 tablespoons chopped parsley
2 tablespoons chopped chives
½ teaspoon Worcestershire sauce
¼ teaspoon black pepper
⅛ teaspoon marjoram
⅛ teaspoon rosemary
⅛ teaspoon thyme
1 clove garlic, minced

Sauce:
2 jars red currant jelly
½ cup butter
½ bottle chili sauce
chopped fresh mint

Veal Scallops with Mushrooms

2 **pounds veal cutlets (pounded to ¼ inch thick)**
1½ **teaspoons salt**
¼ **teaspoon freshly ground black pepper**
½ **cup flour**
6 **tablespoons butter**
2 **tablespoons olive oil**
1½ **pounds mushrooms, sliced**
2 **tablespoons finely chopped shallots or onions**
¾ **cup beef broth**
¾ **cup dry white wine**
1 **large tomato, peeled, seeded and chopped**
1 **teaspoon tarragon leaves, crumbled**
½ **teaspoon savory leaves,crumbled**
½ **teaspoon dry mustard**
2 **tablespoons fresh chopped parsley lime or lemon slices**

1. Mix the salt and pepper with the flour and spread on a large piece of waxed paper. Dip each piece of veal into the flour and coat lightly on both sides, shaking the pieces to remove any excess flour.

2. In a very large skillet, melt 3 tablespoons of the butter with the olive oil until it begins to bubble. Add the veal, a few pieces at a time and cook until golden brown on each side about 2 to 3 minutes per side. Do not overcook or veal will get tough and dry out. Remove browned veal to platter and cook remaining cutlets, adding one additional tablespoon butter as needed.

3. When all the veal has been browned, add the 2 remaining table-spoons butter and saute the mush-rooms until barely golden but still firm. Remove mushrooms and place on top of veal.

4. Put the shallots or onion, broth and wine in the skillet, bring to a boil, lower heat and stir to loosen pieces on bottom. Add the tomato, tarragon, savory and mustard. Add the veal and the mushrooms and the accumu-lated juices back to the skillet. Spoon the sauce over the meat and cook, covered, over low heat, for 30 min-utes, basting and turning occasion-ally.

5. To serve, arrange veal on a warm platter and sprinkle with the chopped parsley. Garnish with lime or lemon slice. Yield: 6 servings.

Note: May be cooked ahead and reheated just before serving. Do not simmer for 30 minutes as stated in step 4 until ready to serve.

Veal Roast

1. Soak mushrooms in warm water for 20 minutes. Drain mushrooms, reserving the soaking water. Rinse mushrooms under running water to dislodge any remaining sand, then chop coarsely. Strain the soaking water several times through a single layer of paper towel. Set aside.

2. In a medium-sized, heavy roasting pan, heat the butter and 2 tablespoons of the oil. Saute the onions or shallots, carrots and garlic for 5 minutes or until the vegetables soften.

3. Remove vegetables from pan and set aside. Add remaining 2 tablespoons of oil to pan and brown the veal roast well. Season with salt and pepper. Add the wine, deglaze the pan to loosen any browned meat bits on bottom of pan.

4. Top meat in roasting pan with sauteed vegetables, mushrooms and mushroom liquid and rosemary sprigs. Cover loosely with foil and bake at 325° for 2 to 2½ hours, or until meat is fork tender.

5. Serve with Risotto Milanese or a favorite rice dish, garnished with chopped parsley. Yield: 4 servings.

1 **(2-2½ pound) veal O-bone roast**
¾ **ounce dried porcini mushrooms**
1 **cup warm water**
4 **tablespoons olive oil**
2 **tablespoons butter**
1 **small onion, chopped (or shallots)**
2 **carrots, chopped**
2 **cloves garlic, minced seasoned salt and pepper**
1 **cup dry white wine**
2-3 **sprigs fresh rosemary, or 1 tablespoon dried rosemary**

Osso Bucco (Braised Veal Shanks)

8 **(2½ inch thick) veal shanks**
2 **tablespoons olive oil**
2 **tablespoons butter**
3 **medium carrots, chopped**
1 **large onion, chopped**
2 **stalks celery, chopped**
2 **cloves garlic, minced**
1 **(28 ounce) can crushed tomatoes with added puree**
1 **cup red or white wine**
2 **cups beef or chicken broth, preferably home-made**
salt and pepper to taste
2 **large sprigs fresh rosemary, or 2 table-spoons dried rosemary**
½ **teaspoon thyme**
1 **recipe Risotto Milanese (see Rice section)**

1. Brown veal shanks well on all sides in oil and butter, in a Dutch oven. Set aside. Saute carrots, onion, celery and garlic in same pan, adding more oil if necessary. Cook until almost browned.

2. Add tomatoes, wine, stock and seasonings, and cook over low heat, covered, until tender, 2 to 3 hours. Or, bake in the oven, covered, at 325° for 2 to 3 hours.

3. Serve on a platter surrounded by Risotto Milanese (see Rice section) and lots of fresh, chopped parsley and lemon wedges. Or, serve in large, individual shallow soup bowls, with rice on bottom, veal shank and sauce on top, garnished with parsley and lemon. Yield: 8 servings.

Pan-Fried Veal Chops

1. Saute veal chops in oil with rosemary in a large skillet (if necessary, use 2 skillets). Cook until brown on both sides. Do not overcook.

2. While chops are cooking, make sauce. In olive oil and butter, saute shallots and apples until tender-crisp. Add brown sugar to taste, port wine and cranberries. Cook until cranberries are tender, but not mushy. (Sauce may be made just before chops are cooked and kept warm.)

3. Remove chops to a heated platter and pour sauce over the top or serve on the side. Yield: 6 servings.

6 **veal chops, 1 to 1½ inches thick, seasoned with salt and pepper**
2 **tablespoons olive oil**
2-3 **sprigs fresh rosemary**

Sauce:
3 **large shallots, coarsely chopped**
3 **Granny Smith apples, peeled and coarsely chopped**
2 **tablespoons olive oil**
2 **tablespoons butter**
1-2 **tablespoons brown sugar**
¼ **cup port wine**
½ **pound whole fresh cranberries**

Red Wine Marinade for Meat

1. Mix all ingredients together. (Can be made in food processor, chopping ingredients until smooth.)

2. Marinate meat (flank steak, chuck steak, or London broil) overnight and grill or broil as desired. Yield: 2¼ cups.

¾ **cup vegetable oil**
¾ **cup dry red wine**
1 **tablespoon lemon juice**
1-2 **garlic cloves, mashed**
⅓ **cup chopped red onion**
1 **teaspoon oregano**
½ **teaspoon thyme**
1 **tablespoon sugar**
1 **teaspoon salt**
½ **teaspoon pepper**
3 **tablespoons red wine vinegar**

Sweet-Sour Marinade for Meat

1 cup soy sauce
1 cup catsup
½ cup sugar
2 tablespoons hoisin
** sauce**
1 tablespoon sherry
1 tablespoon wine vinegar
6 cloves garlic, minced
2 tablespoons fresh
** ginger, peeled and**
** minced**

1. Mix all ingredients together and pour over meat (spareribs, leg of lamb, chicken or fish). Marinate at least 2 hours in refrigerator. For best results marinate for 24 hours. Yield: 2½ cups.

Note: Can be stored in refrigerator, covered, for up to 1 month.

Vegetables

VEGETABLES

The wine match for vegetables depends upon the sauce, but would tend toward lighter, balanced whites (Chenin Blanc, Johannisberg Riesling, Pinot Blanc).

Crunchy Roasted Potatoes

1. Using a large pot, steam the potatoes in 1 inch boiling water, covered, until just tender. Drain and cool.

2. Using steel blade of food processor, process shallots for 20 seconds (or chop finely by hand). Add parsley, salt and pepper and process another 20 seconds (or add finely chopped parsley, salt and pepper). Add melted butter.

3. Cut potatoes into 2 inch chunks and place in 9x13 inch pan. Pour butter mixture over them and toss. Sprinkle with paprika and place optional rosemary sprigs on top.

4. Bake at 350°, stirring occasionally, until golden brown for 1 to 1½ hours. If necessary, brown further under broiler. Yield: 6 servings.

3 **pounds small red potatoes, unpeeled**
¾ **cup chopped parsley**
6 **shallots, peeled (can substitute chopped onions)**
1 **teaspoon salt pepper to taste**
½ **cup butter, melted**
¾ **teaspoon paprika**
2-3 **sprigs fresh rosemary (optional)**

Note: If cholesterol is a concern, drizzle liberally with olive oil instead of adding butter to recipe. Add more oil as needed during baking.

Crusty Baked Potatoes

1. Slice each potato every ¼ inch vertically, down to about ½ inch from bottom. Do not cut all the way down as the bottom half inch holds the potato together.

2. Separate the slices a little bit and drizzle with butter. Bake at 450° for 30 minutes.

3. Sprinkle potatoes with bread crumbs and drizzle with remaining butter. Return to oven and bake 20 to 30 minutes longer. Sprinkle with Parmesan and bake 10 minutes longer. Yield: 4 servings.

4 **medium to large baking potatoes**
5 **tablespoons melted butter**
1 **teaspoon salt**
1 **tablespoon bread crumbs**
1 **tablespoon grated Parmesan**

Spinach Potatoes

6	large potatoes
½	cup softened butter
1	teaspoon sugar
2	tablespoons chopped green onion
¾	cup half and half
1	teaspoon salt
1½	teaspoons dill weed
1	package chopped spinach, cooked and well-drained
¼	cup freshly grated Parmesan

1. Bake or boil potatoes until tender. Mash them with the butter, sugar, green onions, half and half, salt and dill weed. Add spinach.

2. Turn into buttered 2 quart casserole and bake 30 to 40 minutes at 350°. Remove from oven and sprinkle with Parmesan cheese before serving. Yield: 6 to 8 servings.

Note: Can be prepared ahead of time and frozen.

Zucchini-Cheese Bake

4	cups sliced zucchini
¾	cup diced onion
1	cup shredded Jack cheese
1	cup shredded Cheddar cheese
4	eggs, beaten
1	teaspoon salt
½	teaspoon pepper
1	(4 ounce) can diced green chiles
1	(16 ounce) can whole tomatoes, drained and cut up
2	cups cornbread stuffing mix, crushed
2-3	tablespoons butter

1. Combine zucchini and onion. Place in bottom of a greased 9x13 inch baking dish. Cover with half of the cheeses.

2. Combine eggs, salt, pepper, chiles and tomatoes. Pour over zucchini and cheese. Top with cornbread stuffing mix and remaining cheese. Dot with butter and bake at 375° for 40 minutes. Yield: 6 to 8 servings.

Zucchini-Corn Bake

1. Cook zucchini in boiling water (salted if desired). Saute onion, green pepper, garlic and rosemary in oil until vegetables are tender. Add zucchini, corn, cheese, eggs, salt and pepper.

2. Turn into a greased 9x13 inch casserole and bake at 350° for 45 minutes or until firm. Yield: 6 servings.

1½ **pounds small zucchini**
1 **onion, thinly sliced**
1 **green pepper, finely chopped**
1 **clove garlic, finely minced**
pinch of rosemary
¼ **cup vegetable oil**
1 **(1 pound) can cream-style corn**
½ **cup grated Monterey Jack or Cheddar cheese (up to 1 cup may be used)**
3 **eggs, well beaten salt and pepper to taste**

Baked Corn Casserole

1. Mix all ingredients together and place in buttered 2 or 2½ quart casserole.

2. Bake for 1 hour and 45 minutes at 300°. Yield: 6 to 8 servings.

1 **(1 pound) can cream-style corn**
½ **cup corn meal**
2 **tablespoons sugar (or to taste)**
½ **teaspoon salt**
¾ **cup milk**
3 **tablespoons butter, melted**
1 **(2½ ounce) can chopped green chiles**
2 **cups grated sharp Cheddar cheese**

Note: Good side dish for ham or poultry, or as a light supper entree.

Stuffed Eggplant

1 **medium eggplant**
4 **tablespoons olive oil**
1 **onion, chopped**
1 **clove garlic, minced**
   salt and pepper to taste
1 **tablespoon chopped**
   parsley
5 **green olives, chopped**
2 **tablespoons sour cream**
4 **slices Monterey Jack**
   cheese
1 **cup marinara sauce**
½ **pound cooked shrimp**

1. Wash and dry eggplant. Slice off stem and cut in half length-wise. Slice pulp around edge of eggplant ½ inch from edge. Scoop out pulp, leaving a ½ inch shell. Sprinkle shells with salt. Dice scooped-out eggplant and sprinkle with salt. Let stand 30 minutes.

2. Blot liquid with paper towels from shells and diced pulp. Brush shells with 1 tablespoon olive oil and place in an 8x8 inch baking dish. Broil for 3 minutes and set aside.

3. Put the remaining 3 tablespoons oil into a large frying pan and saute onion and chopped eggplant. Add minced garlic and saute until tender. Add seasonings, parsley, optional shrimp, olives, sour cream and ⅓ of the marinara sauce. Mix well and heat thoroughly. Fill shells with the sauteed mixture. Lay two slices of cheese on top of each filled shell.

4. Place under broiler for about 3 minutes, or until cheese melts. Serve with remaining heated marinara sauce at table. Yield: 2 servings.

Note: Commercial marinara sauce may be used.

Elegant Onions

1. Cook onions, covered, in small amount of boiling salted water, until tender. Drain well. Arrange in 2½ to 3 quart casserole.

2. In saucepan, melt butter, blend in flour. Stir in broth, brown sugar, salt, Worcestershire sauce and pepper. Cook until mixture thickens slightly and bubbles. Pour over onions in casserole and sprinkle with paprika.

3. Cover and bake at 375° for 20 to 25 minutes or until mixture bubbles. Before serving, sprinkle with toasted almonds. Yield: 4 to 6 servings.

4	**pounds small white onions, quartered**
10	**tablespoons butter**
6	**tablespoons flour**
2	**cups beef or chicken broth (preferably home-made; if not, adjust salt)**
2	**tablespoons packed brown sugar**
2	**teaspoons salt or to taste**
2	**teaspoons Worcester-shire sauce dash pepper**
½	**teaspoon paprika**
¼	**cup slivered almonds, toasted**

Celestial Onions

1. Melt butter in a skillet and add onions. Cook over low heat until onions are wilted and golden, about 15 to 20 minutes. Stir often while cooking. Put onions in a buttered oval casserole about 2 inches deep.

2. Combine chicken broth, half and half, salt and pepper in bowl. Mix well and pour over onions. Sprinkle with the Gruyere cheese.

3. Dip one side of the bread slices in melted butter and arrange, buttered side up, over onions to cover entire casserole. Bake at 350° for 30 to 40 minutes, until browned. Yield: 6 to 8 servings.

½	**cup butter**
6	**medium to large yellow or white onions, sliced**
1¼	**cups chicken broth**
1	**cup half and half salt and pepper to taste**
¾	**pound Gruyere cheese, grated French bread slices**
⅓	**cup butter, melted**

Rice-Stuffed Tomatoes

¾ cup long-grain white
     rice
6 large tomatoes
½ cup Parmesan cheese
1 bunch basil leaves
1 small clove garlic,
     minced
     salt and fresh ground
     black pepper to taste
     olive oil (3 to 6 table-
     spoons, according to
     taste)

1. Cook rice in boiling salted water for 10 minutes, drain and set aside. Rice will not be completely cooked.

2. Slice ½ inch off tops of tomatoes, saving tops. Remove pulp from tomatoes, discard seeds and place pulp in food processor or blender. Blend with cheese, basil, garlic and salt and pepper. Process until smooth and mix with rice.

3. Drizzle cavities of tomatoes with olive oil and fill with rice mixture. Put in shallow baking dish just large enough to hold them. Drizzle each tomato with olive oil and top with reserved top slices. (Can be made ahead and refrigerated at this point. Bring to room temperature before baking.)

4. Bake at 375° for 15 to 20 minutes, until rice is tender, but tomatoes are not too soft. Serve warm or at room temperature. Yield: 6 servings.

◊ Nutritional information per serving:

Calories 240	Fat .... 12.7 g	Iron .... 2.5 mg
Protein .... 6 g	Cholesterol .... 5.2 mg	Potassium .... 424 mg
Carbohydrates .... 27 g	Calcium .... 159 mg	Sodium .... 141 mg

Broiled Tomatoes

1. Saute shallots or green onions, combine with mayonnaise, cheese and parsley. Spread on tomato slices.

2. Place under pre-heated broiler for 2 to 3 minutes, until lightly browned. Serve as a side dish with fish or poultry. Yield: 4 to 6 servings.

2 **shallots or green onions, minced**
½ **cup mayonnaise (optional: use homemade Basil Mayonnaise, see Salads section)**
¼ **cup grated Parmesan cheese**
2 **tablespoons minced parsley**
2 **large tomatoes, sliced ½ inch thick**

◊ Nutritional information per serving:

Calories	75	Fat	5 g	Iron	0.39 mg
Protein	2 g	Cholesterol	8 mg	Potassium	128 mg
Carbohydrates	5.6 g	Calcium	53 mg	Sodium	168 mg

Sauteed Herbed Cherry Tomatoes

1. Melt butter and oil in heavy skillet. Saute garlic until golden, not browned; add green onions, parsley, basil, dill and salt and saute for 5 minutes over medium heat.

2. Add cherry tomatoes and cook gently for 5 minutes, stirring to coat with herb mixture. Serve immediately. Yield: 6 to 8 servings.

2 **tablespoons butter**
2 **tablespoons olive oil**
1 **clove garlic, minced**
1 **bunch green onions, chopped**
2 **tablespoons fresh parsley, chopped**
2 **tablespoons fresh chopped basil**
1 **teaspoon dried dill**
½ **teaspoon salt**
2 **baskets cherry tomatoes, stems removed**

◊ Nutritional information per serving:

Calories	79	Fat	6.5 g	Iron	1 mg
Protein	1.08 g	Cholesterol	7.8 mg	Potassium	241 mg
Carbohydrates	5.2 g	Calcium	37.6 mg	Sodium	166 mg

Lemon Green Beans

1½ **pounds green beans,**
   cut in 2 inch lengths
 3 **tablespoons olive oil**
 ¼ **teaspoon salt**
 ¼ **teaspoon pepper**
2-4 **tablespoons chopped**
   fresh basil
   juice of one lemon (2
   tablespoons)
 1 **garlic clove, cut in half**

1. Cook beans, uncovered, in boiling salted water to cover until tender-crisp. Drain well and place in serving dish.

2. Season with olive oil, salt, pepper, basil, lemon juice and garlic. Let stand for 20 minutes to blend flavors and serve at room temperature, garnished with lemon wedges. Yield: 6 to 8 servings.

◊ Nutritional information per serving:

Calories 78	Fat .... 5.3 g	Iron .... 1.9 mg
Protein .... 1.8 g	Cholesterol .... 0 mg	Potassium .... 247 mg
Carbohydrates .... 8 g	Calcium .... 69 mg	Sodium .... 72 mg

Calico Carrots

 1 **pound carrots, peeled**
   and cut into ¼ inch
   slices
 ½ **teaspoon peeled and**
   minced fresh ginger
 1 **teaspoon sugar**
 2 **tablespoons butter,**
   melted
 2 **tablespoons finely**
   chopped parsley

1. In saucepan, barely cover carrots with water and boil 10 to 12 minutes until barely tender. Drain.

2. Mix ginger with sugar, sprinkle over carrots. Add melted butter and stir gently. Sprinkle with parsley just before serving. Yield: 4 to 6 servings.

◊ Nutritional information per serving:

Calories 70	Fat .... 4 g	Iron .... 0.04 mg
Protein .... 0.87 g	Cholesterol .... 10.3 mg	Potassium .... 1.1 mg
Carbohydrates .... 8.6 g	Calcium .... 23 mg	Sodium .... 59.1 mg

Carrot Souffle

1. Separate the eggs and beat the yolks and sugar together until light and fluffy with metal blade of food processor. While food processor is running, add half of the flour, then half of the butter, then the remaining halves of flour and butter.

2. Cook carrots in a small amount of boiling water until tender, about 10 to 15 minutes; drain. Add the carrots and then the cheese to food processor while running, processing until all carrots are blended. Stir in the baking soda with a spatula.

3. In a separate bowl, beat the egg whites with an electric mixer until stiff. Fold a small amount of the egg whites into the carrot mixture in another bowl. Then fold the rest of the egg whites into the carrot mixture.

4. Pour into a buttered 7x10 inch pan and bake at 350° for about 30 minutes or until a knife inserted comes out clean. After removing from the oven, top with topping mixture. Serve immediately. Yield: 8 servings.

2 **eggs**
⅓ **cup flour**
¼ **cup sugar**
1⅓ **cups melted butter**
1 **pound carrots, cut into 1 inch pieces**
1 **cup loosely packed shredded Cheddar cheese**
¾ **teaspoon baking soda**

Topping Mixture:
1 **cup chopped walnuts**
¼ **cup sugar**
¼ **cup butter**

Alternate Serving Method: Butter 8 (4 ounce) custard cups. Place a tablespoon of the topping in each cup. Divide unbaked souffle mixture among cups. Bake about 15 to 20 minutes, or until knife inserted comes out clean. Run a knife around the edge of the custard cups and invert on dinner plates.

Optional: Serve with a dollop of sour cream.

Savory Green Peas

2 **(10 ounce) packages**
frozen peas, thawed
¼ **cup butter**
3 **stalks celery, finely**
diced
½ **white onion, finely diced**
1 **chicken bouillon cube**
¼ **cup white wine**
¼ **cup water**
½ **cup sliced almonds**
pepper to taste

1. In frying pan, melt butter and saute celery and onion until crisp-tender. Add bouillon cube, wine and water. Add thawed peas and almonds and blend well. Add pepper to taste.

2. Pour into greased 1½ quart casserole and bake, uncovered, for 10 to 15 minutes at 400°. Yield: 6 servings.

◊ Nutritional information per serving:

Calories	197	Cholesterol	21 mg	Potassium	265 mg
Protein	6.8 g	Calcium	52 mg	Sodium	256 mg
Carbohydrates	15.4 g	Iron	1.9 mg		

Mushrooms and Green Peppers Berkeley

1 **pound fresh mush-**
rooms, halved
2 **medium green peppers,**
cut into 1 inch square
pieces
½ **cup butter**
1 **onion, finely chopped**
2 **tablespoons Dijon**
mustard
2 **tablespoons Worcester-**
shire sauce
½ **cup brown sugar**
¾ **cup red wine**
fresh ground pepper
seasoned salt

1. Melt butter in heavy saucepan and saute onion until transparent. Add the mushrooms and pepper and saute two minutes, stirring frequently. When mushrooms begin to reduce in size, remove from heat.

2. In separate bowl, mix together the mustard, brown sugar and Worcestershire sauce until smooth; add the wine and season with lots of freshly ground black pepper and a little · seasoned salt. Stir well.

3. Add the wine sauce to the mushrooms and peppers and simmer over medium-low heat for 4 to 5 minutes or until sauce is reduced and thickened. Transfer to serving dish. Yield: 4 servings.

Creamed Celery Parmesan

1. Melt 2 tablespoons of the butter in large skillet until frothy. Add the almonds and celery and cover. Simmer over low heat for 15 to 20 minutes, stirring occasionally.

2. Add the remaining 2 tablespoons butter, melt. Blend in the flour and add the light cream slowly, stirring until blended. Add the pepper and chicken broth and cook over moderate heat until sauce comes to a full boil and thickens, stirring constantly.

3. Spoon into a 1 quart buttered casserole dish and sprinkle with Parmesan cheese. Broil until cheese is browned. Yield: 4 to 6 servings.

4 **tablespoons butter**
1 **cup slivered almonds**
3 **cups diced celery**
3 **tablespoons flour**
½ **cup light cream**
⅛ **teaspoon pepper**
1 **cup chicken broth**
3 **tablespoons Parmesan cheese (or more, according to taste)**

Braised Baby Artichokes with Tiny Peas

1. Cut off top third of artichoke and break off all tough outer leaves down to the pale green inner leaves. Trim stem ends, discard and cut artichoke into quarters. To prevent artichokes from turning black, drop into water with juice of 1 lemon for several minutes.

2. Saute onion and garlic in olive oil 3 to 4 minutes. Add drained artichokes and cook, covered, over low-medium heat until artichokes are tender, 10 to 15 minutes. Just before serving, add peas and heat through. Season with salt and pepper and mint. Garnish with lemon or lime wedges. Yield: 8 to 10 servings.

2 **dozen baby artichokes (no larger than 2½ inches in diameter)**
1 **lemon**
4 **tablespoons olive oil**
1 **large onion, minced**
1 **clove garlic, minced**
1 **(10 ounce) package tender, tiny peas, defrosted and drained salt and pepper to taste fresh chopped mint to taste**

◊ Nutritional information per serving:

Calories	133	Fat	5.8 g	Iron	2.3 mg
Protein	4.7 g	Cholesterol	0 mg	Potassium	414 mg
Carbohydrates	19 g	Calcium	62 mg	Sodium	122 mg

Artichokes au Gratin

2 **(8½ ounce) cans arti-
choke hearts**
4 **whole green onions,
chopped (white and
green parts separated)**
1 **clove garlic, minced**
¼ **cup butter**
pepper to taste
¾ **teaspoon salt**
¼ **teaspoon dry mustard**
⅓ **cup flour**
1½ **cups milk**
1 **egg, slightly beaten**
1 **cup grated Swiss
cheese**
1 **tablespoon bread
crumbs**
paprika

1. Drain artichoke hearts, reserving ½ cup liquid. Melt butter in saucepan and saute white part of onion and garlic over medium heat for 4 to 5 minutes. Add salt, pepper, mustard and flour and stir well. Add artichoke liquid and milk, stirring constantly. Cook and stir over medium heat until sauce is smooth and thickened.

2. Remove from heat, add egg by stirring some hot mixture into egg, then adding egg to hot mixture along with half the Swiss cheese. Stir until well blended.

3. Place artichoke hearts in a single layer in a shallow 8x10 inch greased baking dish. Cover with sauce. Combine remaining cheese, bread crumbs, chopped green part of the onions, and paprika. Sprinkle over the top of the baking dish.

4. Bake at 450° for 15 to 20 minutes. Yield: 6 servings.

Desserts

DESSERTS

The three easiest choices for matching California wine with desserts are Late Harvest Johannisberg Rieslings, Late Harvest Zinfandel (high-alcohol Zinfandel made in a Port style) and "California Port," which is a fortified wine made to imitate the styles of the wines of Oporto, in Portugal. The Late Harvest wines are similar in style to Sauternes of France and the Auslese, Beerenauslese and Trockenbeerenauslese wines of Germany. They have a high degree of residual sugar and, in most cases, can serve as desserts unto themselves.

Port goes well with almonds and other nuts, fruit dishes and cookies. The Rieslings go best alone. Sparkling Wine, particularly with higher degrees of residual sugar, work well with fruits, berries and lighter baked goods, such as apple tarts. If the dessert is chocolate, save a little Cabernet Sauvignon to go with it. A secret dessert combination for a group of winemakers in the north coast counties: rich fudge brownies enhanced with chocolate chips and served with 10-year-old Cabernet. Wow!

Chocolate Satin Sin Cheesecake

1. Preheat oven to 350°. Combine wafers and butter in medium bowl and mix well. Pat into bottom of 9 inch spring-form pan. Bake for 10 minutes.

2. Melt chocolate chips in top of double boiler over hot (not boiling) water. Place in small bowl. Mix cream cheese, ½ cup of the sugar and the vanilla in food processor or large bowl of electric mixer. Blend in egg yolks. Add melted chocolate to cheese mixture and blend well.

3. In another bowl, beat egg whites until stiff. Gradually add remaining ¼ cup sugar to whites and beat well. Fold into batter.

4. In another bowl, whip 1 cup of the cream until soft peaks form. Fold cream and pecans into batter. Pour into baked crust in pan and freeze overnight.

5. To serve: remove sides of spring-form pan and slice into wedges. Whip remaining cup of cream. Garnish with whipped cream and chocolate curls. Yield: 12 to 16 servings.

1½ **cups crushed chocolate or vanilla wafers**
⅓ **cup unsalted butter, melted**
1 **(6 ounce) package semi-sweet chocolate chips**
1 **(8 ounce) package cream cheese, at room temperature**
¾ **cup sugar**
1 **teaspoon vanilla**
2 **eggs, separated**
2 **cups whipping cream**
½ **cup pecans, chopped chocolate curls (made with a chocolate bar and vegetable peeler)**

Apple Strudel

**4 cooking apples, peeled
and thinly chopped into
little cubes**
2 tablespoons sugar
1 teaspoon vanilla
**¾ cup walnuts, chopped
finely**
¾ cup sugar
½ cup bread crumbs
¼ pound filo dough
**½ cup butter, melted
sifted powdered sugar
for top**

1. Toss apples with 2 tablespoons sugar and vanilla; set aside.

2. Combine walnuts, sugar and bread crumbs.

3. Carefully lay one sheet filo on a clean dish towel. Brush with butter and sprinkle with some of crumb mixture. Continue to layer filo, butter and crumb mixture until you have used 5 sheets of filo dough, ending with filo on top. Spread apples on half of top filo square.

4. Begin rolling strudel as for a jelly roll from the end that has the apples on top. Gently roll until all filo is into a roll. Carefully lift onto a cookie sheet (if it breaks, patch with more filo/butter). Put seam-side down. Brush roll with butter.

5. Bake at 350° for 45 minutes or until apples are tender and pastry is crisp. Cool; sprinkle powdered sugar on top. Can be frozen and baked the day you serve it; don't defrost before baking, just bake 10 minutes longer. Yield: 8 to 10 servings.

Apricot Noodle Pudding

1. Cook noodles according to package directions, drain and return to cooking pan or to a large bowl. Set aside.

2. In a separate bowl, blend the cream cheese and sugar together. Add beaten eggs and stir well. Add 6 tablespoons melted butter, milk and apricot nectar. Pour mixture over noodles in cooking pot and mix well. Pour mixture into greased 9x13 inch baking dish, and top with apricot halves.

3. Mix together the corn flakes, sugar, and cinnamon and sprinkle over noodle mixture. Drizzle with 6 tablespoons of melted butter. Bake at 350° for 50 to 60 minutes. Do not overbake! Yield: 8 to 10 servings.

½ **pound medium egg noodles**
1 **(3 ounce) package cream cheese, softened**
¼ **cup sugar**
3 **eggs, well beaten**
6 **tablespoons melted butter**
¾ **cup milk**
1¼ **cups apricot nectar**
1 **pound apricots, poached, or 1 (15 ounce) can apricot halves, drained**

Topping:
3 **cups crushed corn flakes**
¼ **cup sugar (or to taste)**
2 **teaspoons cinnamon**
6 **tablespoons melted butter**

Baked California Apples in Red Wine

1. Mix together wine, sugar, red hots and lemon juice. Pour over apples and bake at 350° for 50 to 60 minutes (depending on size of apples).

2. Serve with a teaspoon of sour cream over each apple. Yield: 4 servings.

1 **cup dry red California wine (such as Cabernet Sauvignon or Zinfandel)**
⅔ **cup sugar**
¼ **cup cinnamon red hots (optional)**
1 **tablespoon lemon juice**
4 **baking apples, peeled and cored**
4 **teaspoons sour cream**

◊ Nutritional information per serving:

Calories 309	Fat ....1 g	Iron ....0.5 mg
Protein ....1 g	Cholesterol ....2 mg	Potassium ....223 mg
Carbohydrates ....68 g	Calcium ....19 mg	Sodium ....10 mg

Lemon Mousse

1½ cups sugar
6 tablespoons cornstarch
1 teaspoon unflavored gelatin, in 1½ cups warm water
3 eggs, separated
1 tablespoon butter
4 tablespoons lemon juice
7 teaspoons grated lemon rind
¼ teaspoon cream of tartar
3 tablespoons sugar
1 cup whipping cream
2 tablespoons powdered sugar

1. Lemon filling: Mix 1½ cups sugar and cornstarch in saucepan. Dissolve gelatin in water and gradually add to saucepan. Cook over moderate heat, stirring constantly until mixture thickens and boils. Boil one minute.

2. Slowly pour half of this mixture into slightly beaten egg yolks. Return to hot mixture in saucepan; boil one minute, stirring constantly. Remove from heat. Blend in butter, lemon juice and 6 teaspoons lemon rind. Set aside to cool to room temperature. Pour in serving bowl.

3. Meringue: Beat egg white and cream of tartar until frothy. Gradually beat in sugar, a little at a time. Continue beating until stiff and glossy. Beat in 1 teaspoon lemon rind. Chill in refrigerator until the lemon filling is cool. Gently fold meringue into lemon filling and keep refrigerated until ready to serve, at least 4 hours.

4. One hour before serving, beat whipping cream and powdered sugar until very stiff. Swirl lightly throughout the mousse. Continue to chill until serving. Yield: 4 to 6 servings.

Apple-Cheddar Bake

4 unpeeled, sliced apples
½ cup raisins
1 cup shredded Cheddar cheese
½ cup walnuts
½ cup brown sugar
1 teaspoon cinnamon
¼ teaspoon nutmeg

1. Layer the apples, raisins, and Cheddar cheese in a 9 inch pie plate.

2. Combine the walnuts, brown sugar, cinnamon and nutmeg and sprinkle over the apple-cheese mixture.

3. Bake, uncovered, for 30 to 45 minutes at 350°. Yield: 6 servings.

Friendly Neighbor Flan

1. In a heavy non-iron pan, over moderate heat, melt the sugar and cook, stirring until golden brown. Pour into ovenproof dish (6x10 inches or 8x11 inches) and coat dish well. Place dish in a larger pan of water (about 1 inch of water or enough to reach about half way up the outside of the sugar coated dish).

2. Mix all other ingredients in a blender or food processor until smooth. Pour mixture into sugar-coated dish.

3. Bake, uncovered, at 375° for 35 to 45 minutes or until knife inserted into middle comes out clean. Cool at room temperature and then refrigerate until set.

4. Unmold by placing dish briefly in warm water to loosen; turn onto serving dish. May be made 1 to 2 days ahead and kept covered in the refrigerator. Garnish with orange or strawberry slices. Yield: 8 to 10 servings.

1½ **cups sugar**
1½ **(8 ounce) packages cream cheese**
4 **eggs**
1 **ounce brandy**
1 **(14 ounce) can sweetened condensed milk**
1 **(5 ounce) can evaporated milk**
1 **teaspoon vanilla orange or strawberry slices (for garnish)**

Pear Tart

2 cups flour
½ cup butter
2 teaspoons sugar
½ teaspoon salt
1 egg yolk
⅓ cup water
¾ cup walnuts or pecans
   (¼ cup more, if desired)
⅓ cup sugar
⅓ cup flour
4 large pears (not ripe)
⅓ cup butter
¼ cup sugar
1 cup apricot/pineapple
   jam
1 to 4 tablespoons liqueur
   (Grand Marnier, Kahlua
   or any other of your
   favorites)

1. Mix first 6 ingredients in food processor just until dough forms a ball. Refrigerate for 1 hour.

2. Process nuts, sugar and flour (next 3 ingredients) until they make a fine powder.

3. Remove dough from refrigerator. Roll dough into a 17x12 inch rectangle and place on 15 inch cookie sheet. Make a fluted edge on crust to hold filling ingredients. Spread with nut mixture.

4. Slice hard pears and arrange on nut mixture. Top with cut-up ⅓ cup of butter and sprinkle ¼ cup sugar over all.

5. Bake 1 hour at 400°. Cool. Mix jam and liqueur together and spread over tart to form a glaze. Yield: 6 servings.

Note: This recipe is very versatile. Any hard in-season fruit (i.e., apples, peaches) may be substituted for the pears. Also can be made in a removable bottom tart pan. Bake in upper half of oven so crust does not burn. Great for dessert or as a breakfast strudel.

California Fruit Pizza

1. Prepare pie crust, roll into a 13 inch circle and place on a 12 inch pizza pan. Pinch edge of crust as if for pie crust. Bake at 450° for 12 to 14 minutes. Cool.

2. Prepare custard-cheese filling: In small saucepan, stir together milk and custard dessert mix. Cook and stir until mixture comes to a full rolling boil; remove from heat. Stir in cream cheese and vanilla, using a rotary beater; beat until smooth. Cool 10 minutes, stirring occasionally.

3. Spoon filling into pastry shell, chill 20 minutes.

4. Halve strawberries, slice kiwi and banana. Arrange fruit on top of custard in concentric circles.

5. In saucepan, combine sugar, cornstarch and mace. Stir in juice and jelly. Cook and stir until bubbly. Cook 2 minutes more. Cool. Spoon over tart and chill. Yield: 10 servings.

pie crust for 2-crust pie
1 (4½ ounce) package custard dessert mix
2 cups milk
1 (8 ounce) package cream cheese, cubed
½ teaspoon vanilla
2 cups strawberries
1 cup kiwi
1 small banana
2 tablespoons cornstarch
¼ teaspoon mace
⅔ cup orange juice
½ cup currant jelly
sour cream or whipped cream for garnish (optional)

Optional: Garnish with dollop of sour cream or slightly sweetened whipped cream.

Note: 1 (11 ounce) can drained mandarin oranges can be used instead of the banana.

Holiday Cranberry Cake

½ cup butter, softened
1 cup sugar
2 eggs
2 cups flour
1 teaspoon baking powder
1 teaspoon baking soda
1 teaspoon salt
1 (8 ounce) carton sour cream
1 teaspoon almond extract
2 tablespoons Amaretto liqueur (optional)
1 (8 ounce) can whole-berry cranberry sauce walnut pieces
¾ cup powdered sugar
½ teaspoon almond extract
1 tablespoon warm water

1. Cream butter until smooth and add sugar. Beat 2 to 3 minutes. Add eggs, one at a time, creaming thoroughly after each.

2. Sift dry ingredients. Add alternately with sour cream to batter. Stir in extract and optional liqueur.

3. Pour half of batter into greased tube pan. Spoon cranberries over batter carefully, almost to the edge of the pan, making sure they do not touch the sides of the pan. Spoon remaining batter over cranberries carefully, this time to the edge of the pan. Sprinkle with large walnut pieces, pushing walnuts slightly into the batter.

4. Bake at 350° for 55 minutes. Cool slightly. Combine powdered sugar, almond extract and water in small saucepan and heat over low heat until well-blended. Pour over cake. (You can double the amount of glaze, if desired.) Yield: About 12 servings.

Walnut Torte Cake

1. Cream butter and sugar together; add vanilla, egg yolks, one at a time, beating until fluffy after each addition. Add flour sifted with salt and baking powder, alternately with milk. Pour into 2 greased 8 inch cake pans.

2. Beat egg whites until stiff, then add cream of tartar. Add sugar and fold in chopped walnuts. Spread mixture over the batter in the cake pans. Bake at 300° for 1 hour. Let cool in pans for 10 minutes; continue cooling on racks.

3. Add cocoa and sugar to heavy cream. Let stand one hour, then beat until stiff. Put cooled cake layers together with cocoa-cream mixture and use the rest to coat top and sides of cake. Garnish with walnut halves. Best served the same day made. Yield: 8 to 12 servings.

½ **cup butter, softened**
½ **cup sugar**
½ **teaspoon vanilla**
4 **egg yolks**
1 **cup flour**
  dash of salt
1 **teaspoon baking powder**
⅓ **cup milk**
4 **egg whites**
⅛ **teaspoon cream of tartar**
1 **cup sugar**
¾ **cup finely chopped walnuts**

Frosting:
⅓ **cup cocoa**
¾ **cup sugar**
1½ **cups heavy cream**
  walnut halves for garnish

Applesauce Cake

1. Combine shortening, sugar, eggs and applesauce and blend well.

2. Sift the flour with the baking soda and spices, and add to the applesauce mixture. Blend well and fold in the raisins and/or nuts.

3. Pour into 2 greased loaf pans, or greased 9x13 inch baking pan and bake at 325° for approximately 25 to 30 minutes.

4. Serve with cream cheese for breakfast or tea, ice cream or powdered sugar topping for dessert. Yield: 12 to 16 servings.

1 **cup shortening or vegetable oil**
2 **cups sugar**
2 **eggs**
2 **cups chunky applesauce**
3 **cups flour**
2 **teaspoons baking soda**
1 **teaspoon cinnamon**
1 **teaspoon cloves**
1 **teaspoon allspice**
1 **cup raisins and/or chopped nuts**
  cream cheese, ice cream or powdered sugar as topping

White Cake with Coconut Filling

1¾ cups flour
⅛ teaspoon salt
2 rounded teaspoons
baking powder
½ teaspoon baking soda
⅓ cup shortening
1 cup sugar
1½ cups buttermilk
1 teaspoon white vanilla
1 teaspoon coconut
flavoring
3 egg whites

Frosting:
1 cup sugar
pinch salt
⅓ cup water
1 tablespoon light corn
syrup
3 egg whites, at room
temperature
1 teaspoon white vanilla
1 (7 ounce) can coconut

1. Preheat oven to 350°. Grease and flour four 8 inch cake pans.

2. Sift flour, salt, baking powder, baking soda. Set aside. Combine shortening and sugar, buttermilk, flour mixture, vanilla, coconut flavoring and egg whites, beating well after each addition, until smooth.

3. Divide batter into four pans, turning pans to cover bottom. (Layers will be thin.) Bake about 12 minutes at 350°, until lightly browned. Do not over-bake.

4. Prepare frosting by combining sugar, salt, water and corn syrup in a saucepan. Stir over medium heat until sugar is dissolved and bring to a boil. Cover and cook for 2 to 3 minutes so that the steam may wash down any crystals on the side of the pan. Uncover and cook until the syrup "spins a thread" when dropped from the edge of a spoon (238 to 240° on a candy thermometer).

5. Beat 3 egg whites until stiff peaks form. Add syrup in a thin stream, whipping egg whites constantly, and beating until smooth and creamy. Add vanilla.

6. Ice the cake with the frosting, adding coconut between the layers.

7. Cake layers can be made ahead and frozen. Frost on day cake is to be served. Yield: 8 to 12 servings.

Cocoa Apple Cake

1. Preheat oven to 325°. Grease and flour bundt pan.

2. Cream together the butter and sugar. Add eggs, one at a time and beat until fluffy.

3. Sift together the flour, cocoa, baking soda, cinnamon and allspice and add to eggs and butter mixture. Beat until light and smooth.

4. Fold in nuts, chocolate chips, apples and vanilla, stirring until well blended. Pour into prepared bundt pan.

5. Bake at 325° for 60 to 70 minutes. Let cool in pan 10 minutes, invert and cool completely on rack. Sprinkle with powdered sugar. Great with vanilla ice cream. Yield: 8 to 12 servings.

1 **cup butter, softened**
2 **cups sugar**
3 **eggs**
2½ **cups flour**
2 **tablespoons cocoa, unsweetened**
1 **teaspoon baking soda**
1 **teaspoon cinnamon**
1 **teaspoon allspice**
1 **cup walnuts or pecans, chopped**
1 **cup chocolate chips**
2 **cups apples, grated (2 large Red or Golden Delicious)**
1 **tablespoon vanilla powdered sugar vanilla ice cream (optional)**

Oatmeal Cake

1. Cut the butter into small pieces in large mixing bowl. Add the boiling water and oats. Let stand 20 minutes. Add the sugars and eggs; mix well.

2. Sift together the flour, soda, cinnamon, nutmeg and salt. Add to the oatmeal mix. Add the vanilla and raisins.

3. Pour into greased 9x13 inch pan and bake 30 minutes at 350°.

4. Frosting: Mix brown sugar, butter, milk or cream with egg yolks. Beat until smooth and creamy; stir in coconut. Spread on baked cake and place under broiler until golden brown. Yield: 12 to 16 servings.

½ **cup butter**
1½ **cups boiling water**
1 **cup quick oats**
1 **cup brown sugar**
1 **cup sugar**
2 **eggs**
1½ **cups flour**
1 **teaspoon each: soda, cinnamon, nutmeg and salt**
1 **teaspoon vanilla**
1 **cup raisins**

Frosting:
1 **cup brown sugar**
¼ **cup butter, melted**
3 **tablespoons evaporated milk or cream**
2 **egg yolks**
1 **cup coconut**

Fresh Orange Layer Cake

Cake:
2¼ cups cake flour
1½ cups sugar
2 teaspoons baking powder
¼ teaspoon baking soda
1 teaspoon salt
½ cup vegetable shortening
2 teaspoons grated orange rind
¼ cup fresh unstrained orange juice mixed with ¾ cup milk
2 eggs

Filling:
4 tablespoons sugar
1½ tablespoons flour
dash salt
1 egg yolk
½ cup fresh orange juice
1½ tablespoons lemon juice
2 teaspoons grated orange rind
1 tablespoon butter

Frosting:
3 teaspoons grated orange rind
4 tablespoons butter
4 cups powdered sugar, sifted
dash salt
4 tablespoons orange juice
flaked or grated coconut

1. Sift together into large bowl: cake flour, sugar, baking powder, soda and salt. Add vegetable shortening, grated orange rind and ⅔ cup of the orange juice/milk liquid. Beat vigorously with spoon 50 strokes. Scrape sides and bottom of bowl frequently. Add remaining ⅓ cup orange juice/milk liquid, unbeaten eggs and mix well. Pour into two 9 inch greased and floured cake pans. Bake 30 minutes at 350°.

2. For filling, combine sugar, flour and salt in top of double boiler; add egg yolk, fruit juices and mix thoroughly. Place over boiling water and cook 10 minutes or until thickened, stirring constantly. Add orange rind and butter. Cool. Spread between two cooled cake layers.

3. For frosting, cream together orange rind and butter; add salt and part of sugar gradually, blending well. Add remaining sugar alternately with orange juice until right consistency to spread. Beat until smooth. Frost top and sides of layered cake. Cover with grated coconut. Yield: 10 servings.

Old-Fashioned Chocolate Cake

1. Combine chocolate and boiling water; set aside. Cream sugar and butter; add chocolate mixture and beat.

2. Separate eggs; beat egg whites until peaks form when beaters are lifted; set aside. Beat egg yolks and add milk, cake flour and vanilla. Add chocolate mixture and beat. Fold in egg whites. Finally, add baking powder.

3. Pour batter into two greased and floured 8 or 9 inch cake pans. Bake 40 to 45 minutes at 325°. Cake is done when toothpick inserted in center of cake comes out clean. Cool in pans for 10 minutes, then remove to rack to cool completely.

4. Beat whipping cream until stiff peaks form. Put cake layers together with whipped cream, and use remaining to frost top and sides. Place in refrigerator until served. Yield: 8 to 12 servings.

Note: Instead of whipping cream, other frostings may be used with this cake.

6 **tablespoons sweetened ground chocolate**
5 **tablespoons boiling water**
1½ **cups sugar**
½ **cup butter, softened**
4 **eggs**
½ **cup milk**
1¾ **cups cake flour**
1 **teaspoon vanilla**
1 **heaping teaspoon baking powder**
2 **cups whipping cream**

Pear-Zucchini Cake

2 **cups flour**
2 **teaspoons baking soda**
½ **teaspoon salt**
1 **teaspoon allspice**
  dash nutmeg
1 **cup brown sugar**
1 **cup sugar**
¾ **cup vegetable oil**
2 **teaspoons vanilla**
2 **eggs**
1 **cup nuts, chopped**
1 **cup raisins**
2 **cups grated zucchini**
2 **cups diced fresh pears**
  vanilla ice cream

1. Preheat oven to 350°. Grease and flour a 9x13 inch pan.

2. Mix together the flour, soda, spices, sugars, oil, vanilla and eggs. Gently fold in the nuts, raisins, zucchini and pears.

3. Pour into the prepared pan and bake at 350° for 40 minutes. Let cool and serve with vanilla ice cream. Yield: 10 to 12 servings.

Frozen Strawberry Meringue Torte

1 **cup graham cracker**
  crumbs
3 **tablespoons sugar**
¼ **cup butter, melted**
½ **cup chopped pecans**
2 **cups fresh strawberries,**
  sliced
1 **cup sugar**
2 **egg whites**
1 **tablespoon lemon juice**
1 **teaspoon vanilla**
⅛ **teaspoon salt**
½ **cup whipping cream**
  extra strawberries for
  garnishing

1. To make crust, combine graham cracker crumbs, sugar, butter and pecans; mix well. Press mixture in bottom of a spring-form pan. Bake at 325° for 10 minutes. Cool.

2. In large bowl, mix sliced strawberries, sugar, egg whites, lemon juice, vanilla and salt with an electric mixer on low to blend. Beat on high for 15 minutes until peaks form.

3. In another bowl, beat whipping cream until soft peaks form, add to berry mixture. Pour into crust and freeze.

4. Remove from freezer 15 minutes before serving. Pass extra strawberries at table. Yield: 6 to 8 servings.

Chocolate Cream and Walnut Torte

1. Grease and flour 2 (8 inch) cake pans, fit bottom with waxed paper, grease and flour again. Preheat oven to 350°. Set aside.

2. Beat eggs until light. Add sugar and continue to beat until light yellow. Add and blend in the crumbs and nuts. Divide batter between pans and bake for 20 minutes, or until a wooden toothpick inserted in the middle comes out clean. Cool in pans 10 minutes, then invert onto wire racks. Remove the waxed paper while still warm.

3. For frosting, beat cream until stiff. Mix the chocolate with half of the cream and use this to fill the middle, between the two layers. Use the remaining plain cream to frost the top layer.

4. Make chocolate leaves to garnish the torte: Melt together 1 (6 ounce) bag chocolate chips with 1½ tea-spoons vegetable shortening. Paint chocolate on the undersides of leaves with an artist's brush. Place on cookie sheet and refrigerate until hard. Gently peel away the leaf and discard. Use remaining melted chocolate to drizzle over the top of the torte.

5. Refrigerate torte at least 2 hours before serving. Yield: 8 servings.

4	eggs
1⅓	cups sugar
1⅓	cups graham cracker crumbs
⅔	cup ground walnuts
2	cups heavy cream
6	ounces semi-sweet chocolate, melted
1½	teaspoons vegetable shortening

Flour Tortilla Torte

1 (6 ounce) package semi-
  sweet chocolate chips
2 cups sour cream
3 tablespoons powdered
  sugar
4 (8 inch diameter) flour
  tortillas
1 (2 ounce) piece milk
  chocolate

1. In a double boiler, melt together the chocolate chips with 1 cup of the sour cream and 1 tablespoon of the powdered sugar, stirring constantly. Remove from heat and place the pan of sauce in cold water to cool, stirring occasionally.

2. Set one of the flour tortillas on a serving plate and spread evenly with ⅓ of the filling, then repeat with the other tortillas and the filling, ending with the last tortilla on top. Make as level as possible.

3. Blend the remaining sour cream with the remaining 2 tablespoons powdered sugar and spread evenly over the top and sides of the tortilla torte. Chill, covered with a large inverted bowl, at least 8 hours or as long as overnight.

4. Shave milk chocolate into curls using a vegetable peeler. Pile chocolate curls onto top of tortilla torte. Cut into slim wedges with a sharp knife to serve. Yield: 8 to 12 servings.

Mocha Torte

1. Grease a 9 inch spring-form pan and shake with fine breadcrumbs to coat well. Beat egg whites until stiff. Mix ground almonds with sugar. Gently fold into beaten egg whites. Pour egg white mixture into prepared pan and bake 45 minutes at 350°. Cool pan on rack.

2. Meanwhile, heat water in small pan. Add coffee. Beat egg yolks and sugar and, over low heat, stir into coffee. Beat until thick. Cool and fold in beaten whipping cream.

3. Remove cake from pan. Clean the pan and return the cake. Add the cream mixture. Freeze at least 4 hours. Take out of freezer 30 minutes before serving. Remove from pan and place on serving plate.

4. Put chocolate chips in small plastic bag. Simmer in warm water until melted. Cut small hold in corner and pour chocolate onto cake to garnish. Yield: 8 to 12 servings.

- 2 **tablespoons fine breadcrumbs**
- 4 **egg whites, stiffly beaten**
- 1 **cup almonds, finely ground**
- ⅔ **cup sugar**
- ⅓ **cup water**
- 1½ **teaspoons instant coffee**
- 4 **egg yolks**
- ½ **cup powdered sugar**
- 2 **cups whipping cream, stiffly beaten**
- 1 **(6 ounce) package chocolate chips**

Chocolate Peppermint Torte

Crust:
- 1 cup crushed chocolate wafers
- 2 tablespoons butter, melted

Filling:
- 1 cup butter, softened
- 1½ cups sugar
- 6 ounces unsweetened chocolate, melted
- 2 teaspoons vanilla
- 6 eggs
- 1½ teaspoons peppermint flavoring
- 1 cup whipping cream

1. Stir together wafer crumbs with melted butter and press into a 9 inch spring-form pan. Bake at 350° for 10 minutes.

2. Beat butter until creamy; add sugar and beat until light and fluffy. Beat in chocolate, vanilla and peppermint flavoring. Add eggs, one at a time, beating 3 minutes after each addition.

3. Whip cream until stiff but not dry, and fold into chocolate-egg mixture. Spoon onto cooled crust. Cover lightly and chill 4 hours. May be garnished with chocolate curls before serving. Can be prepared one day in advance. Yield: 8 to 10 servings.

Almond Torte

- ½ cup butter, melted and cooled to room temperature
- 2 eggs, slightly beaten
- 1 cup flour
- 1 cup sugar
- 1 teaspoon almond or lemon extract
- ½ cup slivered almonds

1. Blend together thoroughly the butter, eggs, flour, sugar and almond extract. Pour into greased and floured 8 inch cake pan. Sprinkle almonds on top and bake at 350° for 30 minutes.

2. Serve alone or with a soft custard sauce (recipe below), fresh berry sauce, whipping cream or ice cream. Yield: 12 servings.

Soft Custard Sauce:
- 2 cups milk
- 5 egg yolks
- ⅔ cup sugar
- pinch salt

1. Scald milk in the top of a double boiler. Slowly stir in 5 slightly beaten egg yolks, sugar and salt. Place custard over boiling water. Stir constantly until it thickens. Remove from heat and beat occasionally as it cools. Add 1 teaspoon almond or lemon extract, refrigerate and chill thoroughly.

Pots de Creme

1. Place chocolate chips, sugar, egg, vanilla and salt in a food processor or blender. Heat half and half in saucepan just to boiling. Pour hot cream or milk over ingredients in blender and blend one minute.

2. Pour immediately into 6 demitasse cups or pots de creme cups. Chill several hours.

3. Serve with dollop of whipped cream and a dash of creme de menthe or Kahlua, or garnish with whipped cream, chocolate shavings and cinnamon. Yield: 6 servings.

1 **(6 ounce) package semi-sweet chocolate chips**
2 **tablespoons sugar**
1 **egg**
1 **teaspoon vanilla pinch of salt**
¾ **cup half and half (can substitute whole milk)**

Garnishes:
sweetened whipped cream and creme de menthe or Kahlua, or chocolate shavings (peel a candy bar with a vegetable peeler) and cinnamon

Almond Butter Torte

1. Beat egg yolks slightly in the top of a small double boiler, beat in milk, sugar and butter. Cook, stirring constantly, over simmering water 10 minutes, until custard coats a metal spoon. Remove from heat; stir in instant coffee. Cool completely.

2. Line each of two large cookie sheets with a double thickness of brown paper; draw 8 inch or smaller circles on each.

3. Place egg whites, cream of tartar and 1 teaspoon vanilla in large bowl and beat until foamy and double in volume. Sprinkle in sugar, 1 tablespoon at a time, beating all the time, until sugar dissolves completely and meringue stands in firm peaks (about 25 minutes). Fold in chopped almonds.

Coffee-Butter Cream:
4 **egg yolks**
⅓ **cup milk**
2 **tablespoons sugar**
1½ **cups butter, softened**
1 **teaspoon instant coffee**

Meringue:
5 **ounces toasted slivered almonds, finely chopped**
2 **egg whites**
¼ **teaspoon cream of tartar**
1 **teaspoon vanilla**
1½ **cups sugar**
1½ **cups heavy cream**
2 **tablespoons powdered sugar**
1 **teaspoon vanilla**

(continued on following page)

4. Spoon meringue into the 4 circles, dividing evenly; spread into thin even rounds. Bake in upper ⅓ of oven (they will burn if baked in lower portion of oven) at 275° or until firm, about 1 hour. Turn off heat and let meringues cool completely in oven; overnight is best. Remove carefully from brown paper with spatula or long-bladed knife.

5. At least 6 hours before serving, beat whipping cream with powdered sugar and 1 teaspoon vanilla until stiff. Place meringue layer on a large serving plate; spread with ⅓ of the coffee-butter cream and ¼ of the whipped cream. Repeat with other layers. Swirl remaining whipped cream on top. Garnish with more toasted slivered almonds and chill until serving time. Cut into wedges with a sharp, long-bladed knife. Yield: 12 servings.

Butterscotch Nut Bars

   3 **cups flour**
1½ **cups packed brown**
     sugar
   1 **teaspoon salt**
   1 **cup butter, softened**
   2 **cups walnuts or pecans,**
     chopped
  ½ **cup light corn syrup**
   2 **tablespoons butter**
   1 **tablespoon water**
   1 **(6 ounce) package**
     butterscotch chips

1. Combine flour, brown sugar and salt. Cut in butter and blend well. Press into ungreased 10x15 inch jelly roll pan. Bake 10 to 12 minutes at 350°.

2. Sprinkle nuts over crust.

3. Combine remaining ingredients in small saucepan. Boil 2 minutes. Pour cooked mixture over nuts. Return to oven and bake 10 to 12 minutes or until golden brown. Cool completely and cut into bars. Yield: 48 bars.

Optional: Cookies may be frosted with a vanilla frosting or cream cheese frosting.

Baked Alaska Pie

1. Hull and slice strawberries. Mix with 2 tablespoons of the sugar. Refrigerate.

2. Remove ice cream from freezer and soften at room temperature for approximately 10 minutes. Fill pie shell with ice cream. Place in freezer until ready to top with meringue.

3. Beat egg whites until stiff. Add salt, remaining 3 tablespoons sugar and 1 teaspoon vanilla. (Egg whites should be stiff but not dry.) Spread meringue over ice cream in pie shell. Cover all edges of the crust.

4. Bake until brown at 450 to 500°. Watch very closely, checking after 3 minutes. Cut into wedges and serve topped with fresh strawberries. Yield: 6 to 8 servings.

1 **(9 inch) baked and cooled pie shell**
2 **cups fresh strawberries**
5 **tablespoons sugar**
½ **gallon vanilla ice cream**
3 **large egg whites**
1 **teaspoon vanilla**
 pinch of salt

Note: This can be made ahead and placed in freezer until ready to bake. Different fruits can be substituted for the strawberries.

Toffee Bars

1. Cream together butter and brown sugar. Beat in egg and vanilla. Add flour and salt.

2. Spread dough in a 15x10x1 inch jelly roll pan. Bake at 350° for 15 minutes or until browned.

3. Place candy bars on warm cookie and return to the oven for about 1 minute until chocolate is soft and runny. Remove from oven and quickly spread melted chocolate across top; sprinkle with chopped nuts.

4. Cool and cut into squares. Yield: 3 dozen bars.

1 **cup butter**
1 **cup firmly packed brown sugar**
1 **egg, well beaten**
1 **teaspoon vanilla**
2 **cups flour**
½ **teaspoon salt**
8 **milk chocolate candy bars**
½ **cup chopped nuts**

Brownie Ice Cream Loaf

1½ cups sugar
 1 cup biscuit mix
 ¾ cup chopped nuts
 ¾ cup butter, melted
1½ teaspoons vanilla
 3 eggs
 3 ounces melted un-
    sweetened chocolate
    (cooled)
 1 quart ice cream, slightly
    softened
    powdered sugar

Garnishes:
    whipping cream
    fudge sauce (optional)
    fruit slices for garnish

1. Line jelly roll pan, 15½x10½x1 inches, with aluminum foil. Grease foil.

2. Mix sugar, biscuit mix, chopped nuts, butter, vanilla, eggs and chocolate together; beat vigorously 30 strokes. Spread in pan. Bake 25 minutes at 350°, or until set. Cool brownie in pan on wire rack. Invert on rack or cookie sheet and remove foil.

3. Cut brownie crosswise into 3 equal parts. Place one part of brownie on serving plate, spread with half of the ice cream. Top with another part brownie, the remaining ice cream and the last part of the brownie. Sprinkle with powdered sugar.

4. Wrap in aluminum foil and freeze until firm, at least 8 hours. Remove from freezer 10 minutes before serving. Cut into slices. Garnish with whipped cream and fudge sauce, if desired. Decorate plates with fresh fruit slices (strawberries, kiwi or pineapple). Yield: 8 to 10 servings.

Fudge Brownies

1. Melt chocolate in top of a double boiler. Add butter and stir until melted. Cool 5 minutes.

2. Add sugar, eggs and vanilla and beat thoroughly. Mix in flour, salt and nuts. Pour into greased 9x13 inch glass baking dish. Bake 40 minutes at 300°. Cool 15 minutes.

3. While brownies are cooling, make the frosting. Combine sugar, butter and milk in saucepan. Boil for 1 minute. Remove from heat, beat in chocolate chips. Pour immediately over brownies. Cool and cut into squares. Yield: 2 teenage servings or 18 adult servings.

4 squares unsweetened chocolate
1 cup butter or margarine
2 cups sugar
4 eggs
1 teaspoon vanilla
1⅓ cups flour
pinch of salt (optional)
1½ cups chopped nuts

Frosting:
1 cup sugar
5 tablespoons butter
⅓ cup milk
1 (6 ounce) package chocolate chips

Raspberry-Fudge Brownies

1. Melt unsweetened chocolate and butter in top of double boiler or in microwave oven.

2. Beat eggs until foamy. Add sugar and beat only a few seconds. Add vanilla, salt and chocolate mixture, being careful not to overbeat. Mix in flour, add nuts.

3. Turn into greased and floured 9 inch square pan. Bake at 350° for 30 minutes. (Toothpick should be barely clean when inserted in center of cake; cake will be moist.)

4. While brownies cool, melt chocolate chips with vegetable shortening. Spread raspberry jam over brownies in pan, then melted chocolate chips over the jam. Cool in refrigerator before cutting into pieces. Yield: 18 (1½x3 inch) brownies.

4 ounces unsweetened chocolate
½ cup butter
3 eggs
1½ cups sugar
¾ cup flour
1 teaspoon vanilla
¾ cup nuts (optional)
pinch of salt
1 (6 ounce) package chocolate chips
1½ teaspoons vegetable shortening (not butter or margarine)
8 ounces seedless red raspberry jam

Rocky Road Brownies

Bar Ingredients:
- ½ cup butter
- 1 square unsweetened chocolate
- 1 cup sugar
- 1 cup flour
- ½ cup chopped nuts (up to 1 cup may be used)
- 1 teaspoon baking powder
- 1 teaspoon vanilla
- 2 eggs

Filling Ingredients:
- 2 (3 ounce) packages cream cheese
- ½ cup sugar
- 2 tablespoons flour
- ¼ cup butter
- 1 egg
- ½ teaspoon vanilla
- ¼ cup chopped nuts
- 1 (6 ounce) package chocolate chips

Frosting Ingredients:
- 2 cups miniature marshmallows
- ¼ cup butter, softened
- 1 square unsweetened chocolate
- 2 ounces cream cheese
- ¼ cup milk
- 1 pound powdered sugar, sifted

Note: Freezes well.

1. Bar: Melt butter and chocolate over low heat or in microwave oven. Add remaining bar ingredients and mix well. Spread into a greased and floured 9x13 inch pan.

2. Filling: Combine cream cheese with the next 5 ingredients. Blend until smooth and fluffy. Stir in nuts. Spread over bar mixture and sprinkle with chocolate chips. Bake 25 to 30 minutes at 350°.

3. Frosting: While brownies are baking, make the frosting by melting butter, chocolate, 2 ounces of cream cheese and milk. Beat in sifted powdered sugar until smooth. Set aside.

4. When brownies are done, sprinkle with marshmallows and bake 2 minutes longer. Immediately pour frosting over marshmallows and swirl together. Cool and cut into squares. Yield: 1 (9x13 inch) pan.

Romance Bars

1. Bottom Layer: Cream butter or margarine until soft. Blend in flour, sugar and salt. Spread mixture in even layer in ungreased, 15x10x1 inch jelly roll pan. Bake at 350° for 10 minutes. Top will not be brown.

2. Top Layer: While cookie layer is baking, beat eggs until light and fluffy. Stir in brown sugar, 2 table-spoons flour, baking powder and vanilla. Beat with spoon or mixer until thick and smooth. Fold in coconut and walnuts.

3. When bottom layer is cooked, remove from oven and spread top mixture evenly on top. Return to oven and bake 20 minutes or until golden brown and firm. Do not overcook or cookie will be tough.

4. Remove from oven, cool and dust with powdered sugar or frost. To frost: Combine powdered sugar, vanilla and cream cheese until well blended. Spread on cooled cookie and sprinkle with chopped nuts. Cut into squares. Yield: 3 to 4 dozen bars.

Bottom Layer:
- **1 cup butter or margarine**
- **2 cups flour**
- **¼ cup sugar**
- **1 teaspoon salt**

Top Layer:
- **2 eggs**
- **1½ cups brown sugar, firmly packed**
- **2 tablespoons flour**
- **¾ teaspoon baking powder**
- **1 teaspoon vanilla**
- **½ cup shredded coconut**
- **1 cup coarsely chopped walnuts**

Optional Frosting:
- **1 (1 pound) package powdered sugar**
- **1 teaspoon vanilla**
- **1 (8 ounce) package cream cheese**
- **½ cup nuts, chopped**

Note: A pretty cookie, nice as a dessert for a tea or luncheon.

Pumpkin Bars

1⅔ cups sugar
2 cups flour
1 teaspoon baking soda
2 teaspoons baking powder
½ teaspoon salt
2 teaspoons cinnamon
3 eggs
1 cup vegetable oil
1 (16 ounce) can pumpkin
1 teaspoon vanilla
¾ cup shredded coconut (optional)
½ cup chopped nuts (optional)

Frosting:
1 (3 ounce) package cream cheese
6 tablespoons butter, softened
1½ cups powdered sugar
1 teaspoon vanilla

1. Mix sugar, flour, soda, baking powder, salt and cinnamon together.

2. In mixing bowl, combine eggs, oil, pumpkin and vanilla. Mix until creamy and smooth. Add dry ingredients and mix together until well blended.

3. Fold in optional coconut and nuts. Put in ungreased 15x10x1 inch jelly roll pan. Bake 30 minutes at 350°. Cool in pan.

4. For frosting, mix together cream cheese, butter, sugar and vanilla until smooth. Frost pumpkin cake and cut into squares or bars. Yield: 24 to 30 bars.

Japanese Hard Tack Cookies

1 cup sugar
¾ cup flour
2 teaspoons baking powder
1 teaspoon salt
2 eggs, well beaten
1 (11 ounce) package dates, cut up and floured
1 cup chopped nuts
powdered sugar

1. Sift and mix together the sugar, flour, baking powder and salt. Add eggs and mix well. Add dates and nuts.

2. Spread mixture thinly on a well-greased 13x17 inch jelly roll pan. Bake at 350° for about 20 minutes, or until brown. Cool and cut into bars. Dust with powdered sugar. Yield: About 3 dozen.

Oatmeal-Crispy Cookies

1. Put first five ingredients in a large bowl and mix well.

2. Add the next three ingredients and mix well. Add remaining ingredients and stir with a spoon until everything is well blended.

3. Drop by tablespoons 2 inches apart on ungreased cookie sheet. Bake at 350° for 12 to 15 minutes. Yield: About 9 dozen.

2 cups butter, softened
2 cups brown sugar
2 cups sugar
4 eggs
2 teaspoons vanilla

2 teaspoons baking soda
4 cups sifted flour
1 teaspoon baking powder

2 cups oats
2 cups crispy rice cereal
1 cup shredded coconut
1 (12 ounce) package chocolate chips
1 cup chopped pecans or walnuts

Creme de Menthe Bars

1. For the bottom layer, heat the butter and cocoa in a small saucepan until well blended. Remove from heat and add powdered sugar, egg, vanilla and graham crackers. Pat evenly on bottom of 9x13x2 inch baking pan.

2. For the middle layer, using electric mixer, add the butter, powdered sugar, and creme de menthe. Beat until smooth, and spread on top of the first layer in the pan.

3. Melt together the last ¼ cup butter and the chocolate chips. Spread on top of the second layer. Chill or freeze before cutting into squares. This dessert will melt a little if left at room temperature. Yield: 48 bars.

Bottom Layer:
½ cup butter
½ cup cocoa
½ cup powdered sugar
1 egg, beaten
1 teaspoon vanilla
2 cups crushed graham crackers

Middle Layer:
½ cup butter
3 cups powdered sugar
⅓ cup creme de menthe liqueur

Top Layer:
¼ cup butter
1½ cups chocolate chips

Macadamia Nut Blossoms

4¼ cups flour
2 teaspoons baking soda
1 teaspoon salt
1 cup sugar
1 cup packed brown
  sugar
1 cup butter
1 cup macadamia almond
  butter, found in specialty
  food stores
2 eggs
4 tablespoons milk
2 teaspoons vanilla
1 cup chopped macada-
  mia nuts
  dash nutmeg
  additional sugar
72 chocolate candy kisses,
  unwrapped (optional)

1. Combine all ingredients in large mixing bowl, except chocolate kisses. Mix on lowest speed of electric mixer until dough forms. Shape dough into small balls; roll in additional sugar and place on ungreased cookie sheets.

2. Bake at 375° for 10 to 12 minutes.

3. When cookies are still hot, top each one with a chocolate candy kiss. Press down firmly so cookie cracks around edge. Yield: 6 dozen.

Pineapple-Apricot Cheesecake Cookies

⅓ cup butter, softened
⅓ cup brown sugar
1 cup flour
½ cup chopped nuts
¼ cup sugar
1 (3 ounce) package
  cream cheese
1 egg
2 tablespoons milk
1 tablespoon lemon juice
1 teaspoon vanilla
¾ cup pineapple-apricot
  jam

1. Cream butter with brown sugar; stir in flour and nuts. Reserve 1 cup of this mixture for topping and press the remainder into the foil-lined bottom of an 8x8 inch pan.

2. Bake at 350° 12 to 15 minutes, until slightly browned. Cool.

3. Blend together sugar and cream cheese. Add eggs, milk, lemon juice and vanilla; beat well.

4. Spread crust with jam, top with cheese mixture, spread evenly. Sprinkle with crumb mixture, press lightly. Bake at 350° for 25 minutes. Yield: 12 to 16 cookies.

Greek Orange and Honey Cookies

1. In large bowl, beat oil, 2 table-spoons of the honey, orange juice, juice of lemon and powdered sugar until well blended. Dissolve the baking soda in brandy and add to mixture in bowl. Add cloves, cinnamon, nuts and orange rind.

2. Add flour to make soft dough, about 7 cups. Shape dough into walnut-sized balls or crescents. Bake at 350° for 15 to 18 minutes.

3. Boil sugar, water, cinnamon stick, lemon juice in small saucepan until it becomes the consistency of medium syrup. Add remaining 2 tablespoons of the honey.

4. While cookies are hot, dip into syrup, place on racks and sprinkle with chopped nuts. Yield: About 8 dozen.

Note: These cookies freeze well.

- **3 cups vegetable oil**
- **4 tablespoons honey**
- **1 cup orange juice**
- **2 lemons, juice only**
- **2 tablespoons powdered sugar**
- **2 teaspoons baking soda**
- **¼ cup brandy**
- **½ teaspoon cloves**
- **1 teaspoon cinnamon**
- **1 cup chopped nuts**
- **1 orange rind, grated**
- **7 cups flour (approximately)**
- **3 cups sugar**
- **2 cups water**
- **1 stick cinnamon**
- **2 cups chopped nuts**

Chocolate Meringue Cookies

1. Melt chocolate chips in double boiler. Stir until smooth. Set aside.

2. Beat egg whites with salt until foamy. Add sugar and beat until stiff peaks form. Beat in vanilla and vinegar. Fold in cooled chocolate, plus coconut and nuts.

3. Place by tablespoons on greased cookie sheets and bake at 350° for 10 minutes. Cool on paper towels or racks. Yield: About 3 dozen.

- **1 cup chocolate chips**
- **2 egg whites**
  dash of salt
- **½ cup sugar**
- **½ teaspoon vanilla**
- **½ teaspoon vinegar**
- **¾ cup chopped walnuts**
- **½ cup shredded coconut**

Note: Meringues tend to be a bit temperamental. Weather should not be too wet or too dry. Makes an elegant cookie.

California Date Bars

1¼ cups flour
½ teaspoon salt
1¼ teaspoons baking pow-
der
1 cup sugar
2 eggs
1 tablespoon softened
butter
2 cups finely chopped
dates
¾ cup chopped nuts
1 tablespoon hot water
1 teaspoon vanilla
powdered sugar
vanilla ice cream (op-
tional)

1. Mix flour, salt and baking powder. In separate bowl, add sugar gradually to eggs. Add butter. Beat in dates and nuts.

2. Add flour mixture alternately with hot water and vanilla. Divide mixture into two greased 8x8 inch baking pans.

3. Bake 30 to 35 minutes at 325°. Cool. Cut into 1x4 inch strips and roll in powdered sugar. Serve with vanilla ice cream. Yield: 16 bar cookies.

Note: These freeze well.

Sherried Walnuts

1 cup brown sugar, firmly
packed
½ cup sugar
½ teaspoon salt
6 tablespoons cream
sherry
1 tablespoon grated
orange zest (colored
part of the skin)
2 tablespoons butter
5 cups walnut halves

1. Combine sugars, salt, sherry and orange zest in a large pan. Stir. Bring to a boil over medium heat, add butter and stir to blend well. Remove from heat and add the nuts.

2. Pour the mixture onto a large piece of aluminum foil. Spread out and cool. Break into pieces and store in an airtight container. This is similar to peanut brittle in appearance. Yield: 5 cups.

Note: Freezes well. Makes lovely holiday gifts.

Vanilla Caramels

1. Grease a 9x9 inch pan and sprinkle with nuts, if desired.

2. Dissolve the sugar with half the cream in a heavy pan. Add the corn syrup and cook until the temperature reaches 236° on a candy thermometer.

3. Add ½ cup of the remaining cream and cook to 242° over low heat, stirring often. Add the last ½ cup of the cream and cook to 248°, cooking slowly.

4. Add vanilla, stirring until mixed; pour into greased pan. Allow to cool completely for several hours. Cut into small squares or rectangles and wrap in waxed paper.

Note: It is necessary to cook this candy very slowly, stirring frequently. A candy thermometer is a must.

½ **cup chopped nuts (optional)**
2 **cups sugar**
2 **cups whipping cream**
1 **cup white corn syrup**
1 **teaspoon vanilla**

California Brandy Balls

1. Sift together cocoa and sugar. Combine and stir in brandy and corn syrup. Combine crushed wafers and nuts. Add chocolate mixture and mix well.

2. Shape into 1 inch balls; roll in sugar. Let stand in covered container for several days. Yield: About 4 dozen.

2 **tablespoons cocoa**
1 **cup powdered sugar**
⅓ **cup California brandy**
2 **tablespoons corn syrup**
2 **cups vanilla wafers, finely crushed**
1 **cup chopped California walnuts**

Plums Poached in Port Wine

1 (¾ inch thick) orange
  slice
12 whole cloves
4 cups whole purple
  plums
1 cup California port wine
½ cup sugar
1 cinnamon stick, 3 to 4
  inches long

1. Stud rind of orange slice with cloves and then cut into quarters. Slash each plum on one side to the pit.

2. Combine all ingredients in a saucepan and bring to a boil. Simmer, uncovered, for 10 minutes or less (fruit should just begin to soften).

3. Chill in refrigerator. Yield: 6 to 8 servings.

Note: Better if made 1 or 2 days ahead of time.

◊ Nutritional information per serving:

Calories 148	Fat .... 0 g	Iron .... 1 mg
Protein .... 1 g	Cholesterol .... 0 mg	Potassium .... 200 mg
Carbohydrates .... 29 g	Calcium .... 28 mg	Sodium .... 8 mg

Cranberry Ice

1 pound cranberries
1 teaspoon unflavored
  gelatin, softened in ½
  cup cold water
2 cups sugar
1½ cups water
2 lemons, juice only
4 oranges, juice only
3½ cups pineapple juice
½ teaspoon salt

1. Boil cranberries in covered saucepan with water for 10 minutes. Run through sieve or food mill.

2. Mix dissolved gelatin with sugar, cranberry pulp, fruit juices and salt. Freeze in ice cream freezer. Serve in sherbet dishes. Yield: 12 servings.

◊ Nutritional information per serving:

Calories 188	Fat .... 0 g	Iron .... 0 mg
Protein .... 1 g	Cholesterol .... 0 mg	Potassium .... 164 mg
Carbohydrates .... 4 g	Calcium .... 13 mg	Sodium .... 91 mg

Traditional Persimmon Pudding

1. Mix persimmon pulp, sugar, flour, soda and vanilla together. Stir in raisins and nuts. Pour into a pudding mold, filling only about ⅔ full and snap the lid tight. If you don't have a mold, you can use a shallow (10x6x1¾) inch pan.

2. Bake 1 hour at 350°. Remove from oven, cool 20 to 30 minutes, remove from mold. Wrap tightly in aluminum foil if not planning to serve right away. Puddings will keep in the refrigerator a long time.

3. To serve: Steam pudding by placing (still wrapped in foil) on a rack over a pan of water. Place in 350° oven and steam until heated through. Serve small slices warm with Bourbon Sauce (see recipe at end of chapter); or do not steam and serve cold with sweetened whipped cream. Yield: 8 to 12 servings.

1 cup persimmon pulp
⅞ cup sugar
1 cup flour
1 teaspoon baking soda
1 teaspoon vanilla
½ cup raisins
½ cup nuts, chopped
Bourbon Sauce (see end of Dessert chapter) or whipping cream

◊ Nutritional information per serving:

Calories 197	Fat .... 3 g	Iron .... 2 mg
Protein .... 2 g	Cholesterol .... 0 mg	Potassium .... 205 mg
Carbohydrates .... 42 g	Calcium .... 21 mg	Sodium .... 70 mg

Bourbon Sauce

1 **cup half and half**
1 **cup heavy cream**
½ **cup sugar**
1 **tablespoon flour**
5 **egg yolks**
½ **teaspoon vanilla**
2 **tablespoons bourbon**

1. Combine half and half, cream, sugar, flour and egg yolks in top of double boiler. Cook over simmering water until thickened.

2. Remove from heat; add vanilla and bourbon. Serve warm over pound cake, ice cream, or persimmon pudding. Can be made ahead and gently reheated in double boiler. Yield: 2½ cups.

Lemon Sauce

1 **egg**
½ **cup sugar**
½ **cup butter**
3 **tablespoons boiling water**
  pinch of salt
1 **lemon, juice and grated rind**

1. Beat egg and sugar. Add remaining ingredients. Cook and stir in double boiler until thick. Good served over pound cake. Yield: About ¾ cup.

Note: Warm lemon in bowl of hot water to extract juice more easily. Also, you can restore hard, dry lemons by soaking them in lukewarm water overnight.

Honey-Orange Sauce for Dessert Fondue

½ **cup butter**
1 **cup heavy cream**
¼ **cup honey**
¼ **cup orange marmalade**
1½ **tablespoons cornstarch**
¼ **cup orange liqueur**

1. Heat butter, cream, honey and marmalade in fondue pot on high, stirring constantly until melted and bubbly. Reduce heat to medium setting.

2. In a separate bowl, mix cornstarch and orange liqueur together. Add to cream mixture and continue cooking, stirring constantly until thickened. Set on low heat until serving.

3. Serve with any type of fruit (bananas, pears, pineapple) or chunks of angel food cake. Yield: 2 cups.

Wines

TOM GABLE

Tom Gable, a native Californian, has been writing about wine for almost 20 years. His columns have appeared frequently in numerous travel, wine and inflight publications and been syndicated in more than 300 newspapers throughout the United States. Tom also contributed to "Where to Eat in America," from Random House, and "The Best of San Diego," from Rosebud Books. He has judged at major wine competitions and studied enology both here and abroad. This is an avocation for Tom, who runs one of the west's largest public relations agencies. He lives with his wife, Laura, a CHS associate, and their three children, in Del Mar, California.

Searching for the right California wine — whether to accompany your favorite recipe, for a special occasion, celebration, or just relaxing around the homestead — has become a classic good news, bad news paradox. The good news is that California is producing the greatest range of technically superior, consistent wines in its history, suiting almost every style and budget parameter. The bad news is: how to choose from the thousands of labels staring out at you from the retailers' shelves?

For starters, there are some 600 wineries in California. Unlike France and other countries where a winery typically produces a single wine each year, the wineries of the Golden State tend to issue entire lines of wines. Those at the higher end of the price and quality scale usually limit themselves to creating a limited number of varietals, or wines named after the grapes they are made from (the top five California varietals — and the most expensive — are Cabernet Sauvignon, Chardonnay, Merlot, Johannisberg Riesling and Pinot Noir). These premium varietals can be made into complex wines that serve as great complements to fine dining and the more elegant recipes that follow in this book.

Larger wineries will tend to offer a wider selection from among the 40-odd varietals planted in California, to include those mentioned above plus less expensive or complex wines that sell well (Zinfandel, Green Hungarian, Gewurztraminer, Grey Riesling, Chenin Blanc, Fume Blanc or Sauvignon Blanc and French Colombard, to name a few). These varietals also go well with food, but generally the more straight forward recipes. As noted with specific recipes, the more one-dimensional or two-dimensional wines can be a great match for certain foods (Gewurztraminer with Chinese; Zinfandel with sausage and peppers; Sauvignon Blanc with chicken salad; Gamay Beaujolais, Chenin Blanc and White Zinfandel for picnics).

Then, there are variations on varietals, such as all the "blush" wines (white wines made from red grapes). A dozen years ago, these blanc de noir wines were rare in California. The wines became popular when the white wine boom exploded and the industry found itself short of white grape acreage. So they pressed Zinfandel, Pinot Noir and even Cabernet Sauvignon grapes and quickly took the juice away from the skins, which give color to the wine, to make a white wine, of sorts. The process isn't perfect, so the wines carried a soft pink or salmon hue. But instead of merely filling a gap, these blush wines became immensely popular and endured. The best go well with picnic and other lighter fare; the majority are made for simple sipping.

Most Californians were weaned on generics, a labeling gimmick clever wine marketeers perfected after Prohibition to help sell wine to uneducated consumers. Instead of confusing people with the name of a grape, the labels offered wines named after traditional European districts, or types of wine: Claret (the British name for Bordeaux wine), Burgundy, Chablis, Champagne, Chianti, etc.

The names have specific legal requirements in their own countries. In California, no such laws exist and these generic wines are usually made from blends of the cheapest grapes available. The names don't mean anything except the wine may be the same color as its namesake. Even this small vestige of appropriateness was broached recently when one winery issued a "Pink Chablis" (real Chablis in France is made from 100 percent Chardonnay).

Generics are often called "jug wines," because they are sold in 1.5 liter bottles, and larger. Generic or jug wines are meant for quaffing; use them at a beach party for 100, a wedding reception where more than 25 percent of the guest list includes sorority sisters of the bride and fraternity brothers of the groom, or any other occasion where quantity is the main requirement, not quality. If you must drink wine with Mexican food, use a generic (a good Mexican beer is preferred).

Once you have decided on the type of wine or wines you need as a perfect match for your menu, you can narrow the search by price range, microclimate, geography and vintage date, for starters. In general, there is a relationship between price and quality. Some new California winemakers have tried to go beyond their range, only to find their over-priced bottles gathering dust on the shelves until they are finally marked down significantly or sold in bulk to the discount chains.

Putting a vintage date on wines is more important in Europe than it is in California because of the vagaries of the weather. Vintages vary here as well, but disasters are rare. For example, the past decade in California enjoyed three great years in a row for Cabernet Sauvignon (1984–86) and only two years that fell into the average range (1981–82).

Vintage dating helps you determine the best time to enjoy the wine, within a general range. The less complex white wines and blush wines, for example, are best consumed within one year to 18 months of bottle date. The lighter red wines are good for one to two years. The best Chardonnays are often released as they approach their second birthday because of extra time spent aging in small oak barrels. If the vintage was a good one, fine Chardonnay can evolve magnificently for five to six years. A good Merlot does well in that same time frame. The more complex and intense Cabernet Sauvignon wines can be enjoyed from five to twenty-five years of their vintage date, although some winemakers are attempting to make softer Cabernets for earlier consumption.

Non-vintage wines are meant to be consumed now. Wineries try to create consistent blends and styles so consumers can be confident of the product from year to year. As a general guideline: good wines can improve with age; average or bad wines cannot. Time can't remedy bad grapes or winemaking skills.

This introduction is meant to enable you to look at wines in a broad context and then begin narrowing selections to match your specific needs and personal taste. Guidance from any source other than your own experience should be looked upon as just that: guidance. Taste is personal. Most of us have the same working equipment for wine tasting and analysis (eyes, nose, palate). As within anything else — cooking, art, music, motorcycle maintenance, brain surgery — one gains by personal experience and learning the vocabulary to ease communications.

The brief, general suggestions offered in this cookbook provide you with a range of choices for each category. Use them as rough road maps, then experiment with different routes to arrive at the perfect wine for your needs. For example, a Pinot Noir might be a great match for a fish dish with a red sauce. Or, during the heat of summer, you might serve cold, sliced roast beef with a chilled Gamay Beaujolais or Sauvignon Blanc (season and temperature are two other considerations in your planning). For "bracketing" your preferences in style, as some enologists call it, you can compare Gewurztraminer from Mendocino and the Alexander Valley of Sonoma; Cabernet Sauvignon from Sonoma's Dry Creek and Napa's Stag's Leap area; Pinot Noir from Carneros and the Central Coast; Chardonnay from Carneros and the Russian River Valley; and whatever else strikes your fancy.

Finding the right match or a new one can even be an excuse for entertaining. Invite a dozen friends both to try a few new recipes from this cook book and sample four different bottlings of the same varietal wine. Use four different vintages, four different geographic regions and four different prices. Hide the bottles in brown paper bags and let everyone vote on how well the wine went with the food before unveiling the labels and prices.

Whether in a "tasting" setting or on a random basis, experimenting regularly, as do the great chefs of the world, will broaden your understanding of the best ways to match wines with food. You may also find new combinations to delight your guests. And, with a little diligence in your constant search for enological and gastronomical truth, you might make a slight dent in penetrating the wonderful world of California wines.

Salud!

Tom Gable

THE "WEIGHT" OF WINES

Cuisine can range from light to heavy in its style and impact on the palate. So can wines. The following offers a general guideline to use in selecting appropriate matches for your menu. In addition to mentally "weighing" the main component of the dish, consider the sauces and seasoning as well. For example, a delicate filet of sole poached in white wine might go well with a mid-range Chardonnay. But you will need a deep, oak-aged wine to match a richer cream sauce.

WHITE

Light, Delicate

California "Champagne" or Sparkling Wine (made in the
    methode champenoise, NOT bulk, nonvintage
    from a good winery)
Chenin Blanc
Emerald Riesling
French Colombard
Grey Riesling
Green Hungarian
Johannisberg (White) Riesling (dry)
Sylvaner
White Zinfandel and other "blushes"

Mid-range

California "Champagne" or Sparkling Wine (made in the
    methode champenoise, NOT bulk; both nonvintage and
    vintage dated from a select winery)
Chardonnay (lower alcohol, 12.5 percent and under)
Gewurztraminer
Pinot Blanc (lower alcohol)
Sauvignon (Fume) Blanc
Semillon

Weighty

Chardonnay (oak-aged, higher alcohol, above 13.0 percent)
Pinot Blanc (oak-aged, higher alcohol)

Dessert

Johannisberg Riesling, Late Harvest

RED

Light

Barbera (low alcohol)
Gamay (or Napa Gamay)
Gamay Beaujolais

Mid-range

Barbera
Cabernet Sauvignon (low alcohol, lesser wineries and vintages)
Merlot (low alcohol, lesser wineries and vintages)
Pinot Noir
Zinfandel (low alcohol, lesser wineries and vintages)

Weighty

Cabernet Sauvignon (high alcohol — 13 percent and over; best
    vintages; select wineries)
Merlot (high alcohol — 13 percent and over; best vintages;
    select wineries)
Petite Sirah
Zinfandel (high alcohol)

Dessert

California "Port"
Zinfandel, Late Harvest

MENU AND WINE PLANNING

[* denotes recipes from *Only In California*]

TAILGATE PARTY

* Mexican Shrimp Cocktail

> *Beer*
> *Jug Wine*

* Pozole Soup with Condiments (served in mugs)

* Romaine, Orange and Jicama Salad

* Cocoa Apple Cake

BEACH PICNIC

* Spiced Shrimp and Mushroom Appetizer

> *Gewurztraminer*
> *White Zinfandel*

* California Barbecued Brisket

> *Zinfandel*
> *Merlot*
> *Cabernet Sauvignon*

* Marinated Rice Salad

* Fresh Broccoli Salad

* Brownies

BRUNCH

Mimosas — California Champagne and orange juice

* Pizza Rustica

> *Gamay*
> *Zinfandel*
> *Barbera*

Hard Boiled Eggs

Fresh Fruits

> *White Zinfandel*
> *Riesling*

*Banana Blueberry Bread

Coffee and tea

LUNCHEON

* Cold Avocado Cream Soup

*Artichoke and Shrimp Salad

> *Sauvignon Blanc*
> *Riesling*
> *White Zinfandel*

Miniature Croissants

*Chocolate Meringue Cookies

VEGETARIAN DINNER

* Lasagna al Pesto

* Orange/Onion Salad

> *Zinfandel*
> *Gamay*

*Italian Rolls

* Pear Tart

ELEGANT DINNER PARTY

* Baked Crab Dip

> *Sauvignon Blanc*
> *Riesling*

* Crown Roast of Pork with Apple Onion Stuffing

> *Gamay*
> *Pinot Noir*

* Crunchy Roasted Potatoes

* Sauteed Herbed Cherry Tomatoes

* Lemon Green Beans

* Plums Poached in Port Wine Sauce

INDEX

SAUCES

SEAFOOD

Clams

Crab

Red Snapper

Salmon

Seabass

Shrimp

ONLY IN CALIFORNIA

Children's Home Society of California, 2727 West Sixth Street
Los Angeles, CA   90057-3111

Please send _____ copies of **ONLY IN CALIFORNIA** $17.95 each _____
California residents add sales tax   each _____
Postage and handling   3.00 each _____
                                       Total enclosed $_____

Name _____

Address _____

City _____ State _____ Zip _____

_____ Check or money order enclosed

_____ Visa/Mastercard No. _____ Exp. Date _____

Signature _____

Make checks payable to *Children's Home Society Cookbook.*
Profits received by Children's Home Society
will directly benefit children in need in California.

- -

ONLY IN CALIFORNIA

Children's Home Society of California, 2727 West Sixth Street
Los Angeles, CA   90057-3111

Please send _____ copies of **ONLY IN CALIFORNIA** $17.95 each _____
California residents add sales tax   each _____
Postage and handling   3.00 each _____
                                       Total enclosed $_____

Name _____

Address _____

City _____ State _____ Zip _____

_____ Check or money order enclosed

_____ Visa/Mastercard No. _____ Exp. Date _____

Signature _____

Make checks payable to *Children's Home Society Cookbook.*
Profits received by Children's Home Society
will directly benefit children in need in California.